D1486830

Cuba

Cuba

BY MARION MORRISON

Enchantment of the World
Second Series

Children's Press®

A Division of Grolier Publishing

NEW YORK   LONDON   HONG KONG   SYDNEY
DANBURY, CONNECTICUT

Frontispiece: Havana woman in traditional Cuban clothing

Consultant: Thomas M. Davies Jr., Ph.D., Professor of History; Director, Center for Latin
American Studies; and Chair, Latin American Studies, San Diego State University

Please note: All statistics are as up-to-date as possible at the time of publication.

Visit Children's Press on the Internet: http://publishing.grolier.com

Book Production by Herman Adler Design Group

Library of Congress Cataloging-in-Publication Data

Morrison, Marion
    Cuba / by Marion Morrison.
        p. cm. — (Enchantment of the world. Second series)
    Includes bibliographical references and index.
    Summary: Describes the geography, plants and animals, history,
economy, language, religions, culture, and people of Cuba, the
largest island in the Caribbean region.
    ISBN 0-516-21051-3
    1. Cuba—Juvenile literature. [1. Cuba.] I. Title.
II. Series.
F1758.5.M68 1999
972.91—dc21   98-28173
                                                                      CIP
                                                                       AC

© 1999 by Children's Press®, a Division of Grolier Publishing Co., Inc.
All rights reserved. Published simultaneously in Canada.
Printed in the United States of America.
1 2 3 4 5 6 7 8 9 10 R 08 07 06 05 04 03 02 01 00 99

Acknowledgments

The author wishes to thank the following people and organizations who were especially helpful in the preparation of this volume. In Cuba, the staff of the National Library, Havana, the Ministry of Education and the Montane Anthropological Museum, Rolando Pujol Rodríquez, Dorothy McLean, and the British Embassy, Havana. In London, the staff of Canning House, the cultural office of the Cuban Embassy, and the staff of the library and map room of the Royal Geographical Society.

Cover photo:
Trinidad

Contents

Havana

Cuban schoolchildren

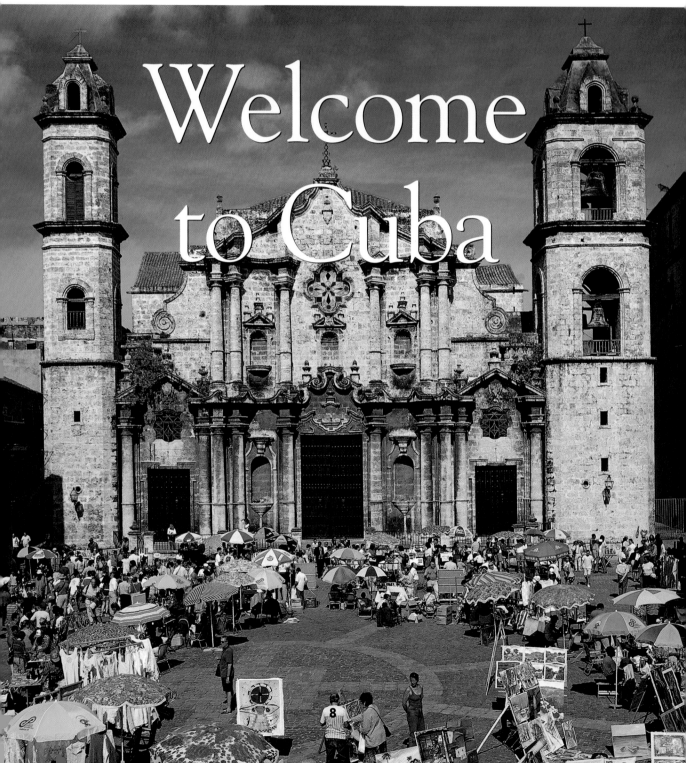

Welcome to Cuba

EVERYWHERE IN CUBA—IN EVERY TOWN, VILLAGE, PARK, schoolyard, and most homes—there is a monument, statue, sculpture, painting, poster, or photo of a great Cuban hero: José Martí. He is known to Cubans as the "father of their nation" and is described as the "most universal of all Cubans." Martí was a poet, a writer, a journalist, a teacher, a philosopher, and a lawyer. But above all, he was the man who inspired Cubans to think of themselves as an independent nation.

Opposite: **Cubans and tourists gather at a market in Cathedral Plaza, Havana**

José Martí, the man considered to be the hero of Cuban independence

José Martí was born in 1853. As a fifteen-year-old student, he began his crusade against Spanish colonialism, working in Havana for the anticolonial newspaper *The Free Fatherland*. In 1869, he was arrested on charges of treason and sentenced to six years hard labor in a stone quarry. After six months he was pardoned but sent into exile.

Martí went to Spain, where he graduated from law school. After that, he was constantly on the move—across Europe, to Central America and Mexico, on secret visits to Cuba, and into the United States and South America. Eventually, in 1881, he settled in New York with his wife and family. At first happy with the freedom the

United States could provide, he gradually became disillusioned. He argued passionately against the United States having any control over Cuba and spread his message among other Cuban exiles. Always distinctively dressed in a black suit and a bow tie, Martí declared to his audiences that *Cuba Libre* (Free Cuba) could never be part of the United States. He urged independence for Cuba, stressing the need for democracy, social justice, and racial equality. Martí was killed in Cuba soon after the fighting against Spain began in 1895.

Cuba became an independent republic in 1902, but U.S. business interests and investment controlled the island's economy until the 1960s. During this time, Cuba was ruled both by elected governments and by harsh dictators. The dictator Fulgencio Batista had effectively held power either as president or indirectly as head of the army since the 1930s, and in 1952 he overthrew the government and returned to power. A small group of rebels led by Fidel Castro determined to defeat Batista, and on January 1, 1959, he was forced to flee the island.

Cuba attracted many American tourists in the 1950s. These vacationers visit Cathedral Plaza, one of the oldest centers of Western civilization.

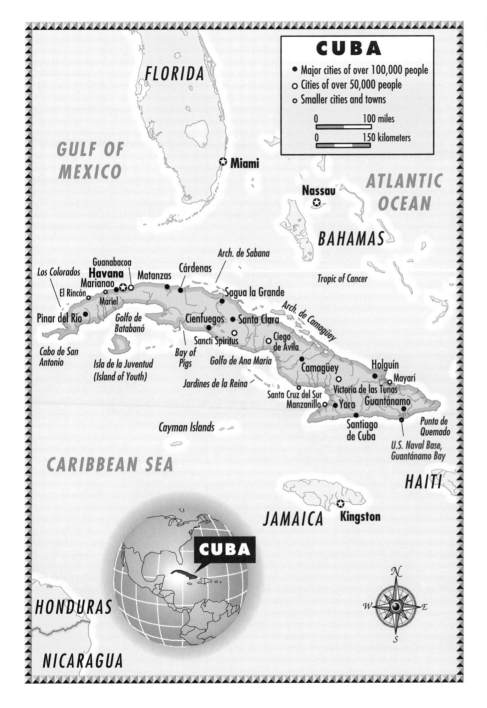

CUBA

- Major cities of over 100,000 people
- ○ Cities of over 50,000 people
- ○ Smaller cities and towns

```
0          100 miles
0          150 kilometers
```

FLORIDA

GULF OF
MEXICO

✪ Miami

ATLANTIC
OCEAN

Nassau
✪

BAHAMAS

Tropic of Cancer

Los Colorados
Guanabacoa
Havana   Cárdenas
Marianao   Matanzas
El Rincón
Mariel   Sagua la Grande
Pinar del Río
Golfo de   Cienfuegos   Santa Clara
Batabanó
Arch. de Sabana
Arch. de Camagüey
Sancti Spíritus   Ciego
de Ávila
Cabo de San   Bay of
Antonio   Isla de la Juventud   Pigs   Golfo de Ana María
(Island of Youth)
Jardines de la Reina
Camagüey   Holguín
Mayarí
Victoria de las Tunas
Santa Cruz del Sur   Guantánamo
Manzanillo   Yara
Cayman Islands
Santiago   Punta de
de Cuba   Quemado
U.S. Naval Base,
Guantánamo Bay

CARIBBEAN SEA

HAITI

JAMAICA   Kingston

CUBA

HONDURAS

NICARAGUA

N
W   E
S

Castro is happy to acknowledge Martí's inspiration and place in the Revolution, and from a very early age Cuban children learn about the moral and social values Martí taught. His poems for children, now set to music, are sung in all the schools. But has the Revolution accomplished all that Martí wished?

A visitor flying into the José Martí Airport in Havana sees below a beautiful Caribbean island, with white sand beaches, tropical palms, and a blue-green sea. The land, once densely forested, has been cleared for sugarcane plantations and cattle ranches. The drive into Havana, however, leaves an impression of a once-beautiful city that is now run-down and in need of more than a new coat of paint.

Maguana Beach in Guantánamo

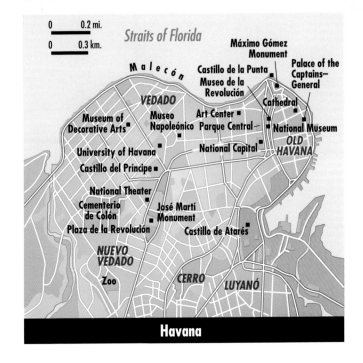

Havana

Havana: Did You Know This?

Population: 2,175,995 (1993)

Year Founded: 1515, by Diego Velásquez

Altitude: 200 feet (60 m)

Average Daily Temperature: 72°F (22°C) in January; 82°F (28°C) in July

Average Annual Rainfall: 48 inches (122 cm)

Havana in many ways encapsulates Cuba's history. The old colonial part of the city is close to the docks. Here stand the forts that once protected the city from pirates, the fine cathedral begun in 1748, and the governors' palace. Recently named a UNESCO heritage site, colonial Havana is being restored to its former glory with houses painted in pastel colors and cobbled streets.

The middle section of the city extends along the coast, separated from the sea by a promenade—the Malecón. In this part of Havana, large mansions and once-fashionable hotels line wide avenues. Untouched for the last thirty years, and with no modern high-rise buildings to spoil the view,

The restoration of colonial Havana includes cobbled streets and pastel houses.

some areas have remained as perfect examples of turn-of-the-century and art deco architecture. Toward the city outskirts are new housing projects that have been built since the Revolution.

Martí said that "to be educated is the only way to be free," and the revolutionary government's spending priorities have been education and health, not building. Today, free education and life-time medical help are available to all Cubans.

Soon after the Revolution, Cuba and the United States disagreed and the Soviet Union stepped in. Cuba became a communist state and relied heavily on the Soviet Union. The United States retaliated with an economic embargo that prohibited trade between Cuba and the United States. With the collapse of the Soviet Union in 1991, Cuba for the first

time became a truly free nation, not dependent on any other country. But the lack of Soviet economic support and the tightening of the U.S. embargo in the 1990s have made life very tough for most Cubans.

Cubans are among the most cheerful, patient, resilient, and outgoing people on earth. They are very generous with the little they have, and everyone who visits Cuba comes away with a sense of warmth and admiration for its people. Their greatest exuberance is in their music, much of which derives from their African roots. Martí himself is remembered in one of Cuba's best-known songs. Words from his *Versos Sencillos* (*Simple Verses*; 1891) were incorporated into the now famous *Guantanamera*:

Yo soy un hombre sincero	I am a sincere man
de donde crece la palma	from where the palms grow
y antes de morirme quiero echar	and before I die I wish to shed
mis versos del alma.	these verses of the soul.

What the future holds for Cuba is uncertain. Fidel Castro celebrated his seventieth birthday in 1996, and Cuban exiles in Florida and elsewhere await their chance to return to the island and restore it to a democratic, noncommunist state. Many exiles have lived outside Cuba for nearly forty years, but they still have great devotion to and respect for José Martí. His name is at the forefront of the Cuban exiles' anti-Castro campaign, broadcast through their U.S.-based Radio Martí and TV Martí stations.

A Grand Island

A community in Punta Gorda, Cienfuegos

CUBA IS THE LARGEST ISLAND IN THE WEST INDIES AND one of the most beautiful. With more than 1,600 smaller islands and cays, or coral reefs, it is officially known as the Republic of Cuba. The nearest mainland is southern Florida. Key West, at the tip of the Florida Keys, is only 90 miles (145 km) away.

The main island lies in a roughly east–west position between the Atlantic Ocean and Caribbean Sea. Jamaica is 91 miles (146 km) to the south, and the island of Hispaniola, which includes the Dominican Republic and Haiti, is just 54 miles (87 km) to the east. This group of islands together with the U.S. territory of Puerto Rico make up the major part of the group known as the Greater Antilles in the West Indies.

Opposite: **A stream on the Isla de la Juventud, or the Island of Youth**

Geographical Features

Area: 42,804 square miles (110,861 sq km); the sixth-largest island in North America and the largest island in the Caribbean Sea

Highest Elevation: Pico Turquino, 6,542 feet (1,994 m)

Lowest Elevation: Sea level along the coast

Coastline: 2,100 miles (3,380 km)

Longest River: Cauto River, 155 miles (249 km)

Highest Annual Precipitation: More than 70 inches (178 cm) in the mountains

Lowest Annual Precipitation: 40 inches (102 cm) in the lowlands

Highest Temperature Extreme: 100°F (38°C) in the southeastern lowlands

Lowest Temperature Extreme: 40°F (4°C) in the northwestern mountains

Greatest Distance Northwest to Southeast: 708 miles (1,139 km)

Greatest Distance North to South: 135 miles (217 km)

Origins

The islands of the West Indies are all that remain of an ancient land that once connected the continents of North America and South America. They are the tops of submerged mountains that stood far above the Earth's surface 3 million years ago. In many places, the older base rocks are overlaid with geologically younger rocks.

Earth's crust is made up of seven large plates and many smaller ones. These plates carry the continents and oceans. The slow, relentless movement of the plates caused the base rocks in this region to gradually dip below the sea, leaving the island chain of modern times.

Cuba is 708 miles (1,139 km) long from northwest to southeast. At its widest point, the island is 135 miles (217 km), from north to south. At its narrowest point, in the west, Cuba is only 25 miles (40 km) wide. Its total land area is slightly smaller than the state of Ohio.

The main island is usually divided into two distinct geographical zones—the western-central region and the eastern region. Almost three-quarters of the island is low-lying, with large plains and river basins. Mountains and ranges of hills reaching heights touching 6,542 feet (1,994 m) are found in the east in the Sierra Maestra. Ranges in the central-south region known as the Macizo de Guamuhaya are lower and those in the west—the Cordillera, or "chain," de Guaniguanico—are lower still.

Looking at Cuban Cities

Santiago de Cuba lies on Cuba's southern coast. Founded by Diego Velásquez in 1514, Santiago served as Cuba's capital until 1553. In 1953, Fidel Castro attacked the barracks at Moncada in Santiago, starting the revolution against Batista. Today, Santiago, Cuba's second-largest city, is a seaport that ships sugar, rum, and tobacco products, as well as iron, manganese, and copper ore from Cuba. Highlights of a tour of the city include Parque Céspedes, Morro Castle, San Juan Hill, and the Caney Rum Factory—the oldest in Cuba. Santiago has some of Cuba's highest temperatures, although the average summer temperature is about 80°F (27°C). Annual precipitation is 40 inches (102 cm).

Camagüey, Cuba's third-largest city, overlooks a large plain in the middle of Camagüey Province in central Cuba. Founded in 1515 as Santa María del Puerto del Príncipe by Diego Velásquez, the city was renamed in 1903 after a Native American chief. The city has become a center for communications, trade, and industry, mainly processing and shipping livestock and sugar. Because the early city did not have a source of fresh water, Spanish potters made huge earthenware jugs, called *tinajones*, to collect rainwater. The city's twisting, turning streets often surprise visitors. Row houses built in the 1700s, each painted a different color, may appear around one corner, while another street may end in a large plaza surrounded by museums and churches.

A mountain range near Baracoa

Granma Province

The province of Granma in eastern Cuba is named after the small vessel that carried Fidel Castro and eighty-one companions from Mexico to start their revolutionary campaign in 1956.

Granma Province is Cuba's fifth-largest province and covers an area of low, fertile plains watered by the Cauto and Bayamo Rivers. The southern part is higher and includes part of the Sierra Maestra range. The coast includes numerous cays such as the Balandras and Manzanillo. On shore the land is varied, with swamps at the mouth of the Cauto and beaches with small coves leading to tiny Hicaco Point on the southern coast.

The Mountains

Cuba's most impressive mountains, the Sierra Maestra, run along the edge of the south coast overlooking the Caribbean in the east. Several parallel ranges form the Sierra Maestra, of which the Cordillera de Turquino is the greatest. The ranges are narrow and steep, so the ascent to the highest point, Pico Turquino (6,542 ft [1,994 m]), is rugged. Another mountain range, the Cordillera de la Gran Piedra, is so named because it is topped by huge *piedras* (limestone boulders). The largest boulder, known as La Gran Piedra, is 82 feet (25 m) high.

At the foot of the mountains, the ancient upheavals of Earth's crust have left an extraordinary undersea slope. Just offshore, the mountainside continues downward for almost 23,000 feet (7,010 m) into the *Fosa* (Trough) of the Oriente. This depth is reached within 13 miles (21 km) of Pico Turquino. The total vertical distance is almost the height of Mount Everest, the world's highest peak.

The Sierra has an important place in the modern history of Cuba. Its cloud-soaked forests sheltered Fidel Castro and his band of young rebels as they began their fight against the government in 1956.

In the central region of the island and to the south are the *Macizo de Guamuhaya* (Escambray Mountains). These are some of the oldest rocks in Cuba, which reached their present form over eons. A few summits rise more than 3,800 feet (1,160 m) and the highest is Pico San Juan. Roads lead to villages in the higher parts. The region is used for farming.

At the western end of the island, the scenery of the Viñales Valley could not be more different. It is typically *karst*, a region of eroded limestone where isolated *mogotes* (hummocks) stand above the plains like enormous rounded loaves of bread. Viñales is one of the island's most beautiful valleys and attracts tens of thousands of tourists every year. Spanish settlers planted vines for grapes in the rich soil between the limestone hummocks. These are the vines that gave the valley its name. Cuba's finest tobacco now comes from this region.

A landscape with *mogotes* in Pinar del Río, Viñales Valley

A farmhouse in the Pinar del Río province of the Viñales Valley

The mountains here are lower but the scenery is rugged. Overlooking the Atlantic, the Cordillera de Guaniguanico reaches only 2,293 feet (699 m) at its summit, known as the Pan de Guajaibón.

Although the scenery varies, limestone is found in about 65 percent of the country. Limestone is a rock composed largely of the element calcium. It is eroded or dissolved by water that contains carbonic acid, naturally formed from the carbon dioxide in the air. The action of the slightly acidic water over millions of years has left many openings or caves throughout much of Cuba.

Rivers

The narrow width of the island limits the size of Cuba's rivers. The longest, at 155 miles (249 km), is the Cauto River, in eastern Cuba. The Cauto is joined in the lower part of its course by the Bayamo River, which rises in the Sierra Maestra, and the Salado River, which begins in Holguín Province to the north. The basin drained by the Cauto is the largest in the country. A dam that was constructed across the Cauto River in 1966 supplies water for Santiago de Cuba, the main city in the eastern end of the island.

Among the many smaller rivers is the Almendares, which flows into the eastern end of the Gulf of Mexico a few miles from the central part of Havana. Havana is Cuba's capital city. The Almendares rises in the hills south of Havana, and flows only 31 miles (50 km). Along the way, it picks up household and industrial wastes. Steps are now being taken to control the pollution, but it may take years to revitalize the river.

Land of Caves

The western end of Cuba is riddled with caves including the largest of all, the Great Cavern of Santo Tomás. This immense cave, with more than 27 miles (44 km) of passages, is in the Sierra de Quemados, part of the Sierra de los Organos in the Guaniguanico range. The cave entrance leads into a maze of six levels with more than fifty separate caves. One of these, the Escaralata Cavern, is filled with a fine crystalline formation made up of calcium-containing minerals. The Santo Tomás River and its tributary, El Peñate, flow through the lower levels.

Cuba's deepest cave is found in the Macizo de Guamuhaya. There, a Cuban-Hungarian expedition located the system known as the Cuba-Magyar Abyss, which reaches a depth of 1,279 feet (390 m). At the bottom, the explorers discovered that the way ahead was blocked by an active system of rivers that led to submerged tunnels. These flooded passages have impeded the full survey of the system. Many of the island's caves show traces of ancient habitation—sometimes by early people and often by wildlife.

Islands, Islets, and Cays

The main island of Cuba has a coastline of 2,100 miles (3,380 km). It is surrounded by four groups of cays and smaller islands. Los Colorados includes 150 cays in the northwest. The Sabana-Camagüey Archipelago of approximately 2,500 islets and keys is on the northern coast. To the south and slightly east is the group known as *Jardines de la Reina* (the Queen's Gardens), with 661 cays and islets. In the south, Los Canarreos Archipelago includes Cuba's second-largest island, *Isla de la Juventud* (Island of Youth).

El Túnel del Amor, or the Tunnel of Love, on the Isla de la Juventud

Harvesting grapefruit on the Isla de la Juventud

Barns made of dried leaves in tobacco fields of the Viñales Valley

Isla de la Juventud has had a colorful history and many different names. Columbus called it *La Evangelista*. Later, it was known as Treasure Island because pirates thought treasure was buried there, and as Parrot Island, after the colorful birds that lived there. The Spanish knew it as *Colonia Reina Amalia*, and in the nineteenth century it was used as a place of exile for criminals and deposed politicians and named *Isla de los Deportados*. It was next known as the Isle of Pines. Finally, it became the Island of Youth to acknowledge the work of the young people who volunteered to live and study there in the 1960s and 1970s. They built schools and created large citrus plantations on the island.

A Tropical Island

Cuba's tropical climate, seasonal rainfall, and low-lying land influenced the original vegetation of the island. Today, Cuba is devoted to agriculture, so the vegetation is changing. While much of the original forest has been cut down, extensive wooded areas remain, particularly in the Sierra Maestra. There are also large swamps where the land is flooded for much of the year.

Hurricanes and cyclones, the most notorious weather events of the region, sometimes seriously affect Cuba. The most recent hurricane to devastate parts of the island was Hurricane Lili in October 1996. The storm formed in the Gulf of Mexico and swept toward Cuba, touching the Island of Youth and then crossing the central region. Large plantations of sugarcane were flattened, some houses were damaged, trees were toppled in the Macizo de Guamuhaya, and flooding affected even the larger towns.

The Hurricane of 1932

The immense energy in the wind of a major tropical cyclone also affects the sea. Huge waves may be created when the level of the sea rises and the wind pushes it forward at high speed. The hurricane of 1932 created waves more than 16 feet (5 m) high that swept inland and destroyed the small fishing town of Santa Cruz in southern Camagüey Province. Thousands of people died, and it was many years before the area recovered. A new town of Santa Cruz del Sur was built 1.2 miles (2 km) away from the old site.

Other devastating storms include Hurricane Flora in October 1963, which affected eastern Cuba. More than 1,200 people died and a wide agricultural area was severely damaged.

Men stand along the sea wall of Malecón boulevard as waves are whipped up by Hurricane Lili on October 18, 1996.

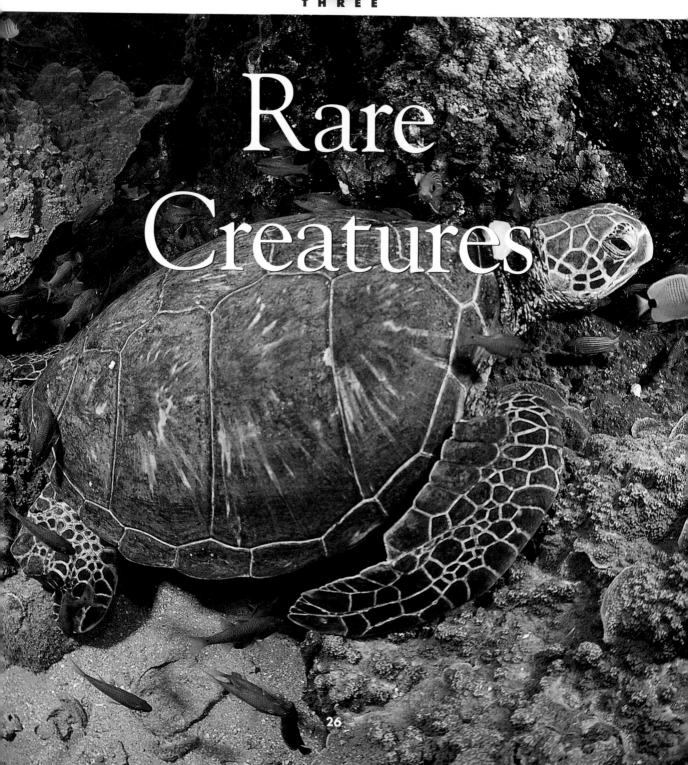

Rare Creatures

WHEN THE ISLAND OF CUBA WAS DISCOVERED BY Europeans, much of the land was covered with forests of cedars and pines. Other areas were savannas—open grassland studded with palm trees. Parts of the coast were lined with large swamps.

Opposite: **A green sea turtle**

Cuba has many brightly colored parrots.

In the large bay of Cienfuegos on the south coast, sea turtles gathered by the thousands to browse on seaweed. The early Native Americans captured the turtles by grasping the sucker-fishes that attached themselves to their shells. Birds were numerous, and early travelers remarked on the parrots and the brightly colored macaws known as *guacamayos.*

Today, the landscape has changed. The last macaw in Cuba was caught a hundred years ago. The brilliant red and green feathers of the macaw were in huge demand in nineteenth-century Europe, and the trade depleted many species in the Americas.

Four centuries of agriculture have made changes too. The palm-covered savannas have given way to immense farm fields. Land has been drained, and much of the forest has been cleared. The greatest decline of the forests began in the nineteenth century and continues today. Replanting programs are beginning to take effect, however. Wildlife is now mostly concentrated in reserve areas where the animals are protected for future generations.

Palm trees line the streets before the Tunnel of Love on the Isla de la Juventud.

Trees and Flowers

The island has a large variety of plants. Some arrived as drifters from other lands, washed along on ocean currents. Others came by animal dispersal. And some, including citrus fruits and cereals, were brought by Europeans.

Plants that have been in Cuba for a long time include a tree called the cork palm—a living relic of the Earth of 65 million to 125 million years ago. The cork palm is very rare and can be seen in only a few places in the western provinces. More than 8,000 plant species grow in Cuba, giving the island a marvelous variety of plant life. Half the species are endemic— they can be found only in Cuba.

Trees and other plant life grow in different regions depending on the altitude, humidity, and soil. The Sierra Maestra has remnants of rain forest with trees such as the crabwood, alligator wood, and the Santa María. These warm, wet forests are filled with ferns and *epiphytes*—plants that grow on other plants.

Coffee farming has altered many parts of these forests because the larger trees provide ideal shade for the coffee bushes. Pines grow in the drier, sandy soil around the Sierra Maestra and cover large areas in other places such as *Pinar del Río* (Pine Grove of the River).

Thorny forests are found in drier regions such as the open limestone slopes and some coastal areas. Many of the plants are *leguminous*, or pod-bearing, with tough, small leaves. Mangrove forests, with their strange clusters of roots, are also abundant in coastal areas, especially in the regions with large *ciénagas* (tidal lagoons). The Zapata *ciénaga* is particularly famous for its mangroves.

National Symbols from Nature

Cuba's national tree is the elegant royal palm, which grows almost 60 feet (18 m) tall. Tens of thousands of royal palms grace the island. The tree's botanical name is *Roystonea*, for General Roy Stone of the United States. The royal palm appears on the national shield.

The national bird is the Cuban trogon. This brilliant bird is red and blue, with white plumage on its breast. The Cuban trogon is found in most parts of the island, and for Cubans it recalls the colors of their flag.

Curiously, the Cuban national flower is the butterfly jasmine—from India! It was brought to the island and used as a kind of secret code among women who helped with the nineteenth-century Independence Movement. Legend says that messages written on slips of paper were rolled up and carried in the flowers. The jasmine grows in many colors, and the white variety is the national flower. Other colors are used in wedding bouquets and church decorations.

The Cuban *hutía* is an uncommon nocturnal rodent.

Animal life in Cuba has its origins in the way the island was colonized. Some species, such as the *hutía*, are relics of the time when a land bridge connected North America and South America. The *hutía* is a rodent related to rats and porcupines. These curious 8-inch (20-cm)-long nocturnal animals have a prehensile tail that can wrap around branches. They have been reduced in numbers by cats and dogs and are now quite rare.

Another strange animal is the tiny, ratlike solenodon, locally known as the *almiquí*, and related to the shrew. This 12-inch (30-cm)-long mammal has a tail that is almost as long as its body, and a long snout. It feeds on insects and other inverte-

The solenodon is one of the world's rarest animals.

brates. The Cuban solenodon, one of the world's rarest animals, is found in the Holguín region where it is protected by law. The only other species of solenodon is found in neighboring Haiti.

Some mammals arrived by simply flying in. Cuba has twenty-seven species of bats. Other mammals, such as the manatee, or "sea cow," arrived by sea. They are found in many tropical waters, especially estuaries and lagoons. The first European sailors in the region thought manatees were mermaids. When Columbus reached the Antilles, he recorded that "three mermaids stood up, out of the sea."

Although there are relatively few species of mammals on the island, there are more than 100 species of reptiles. Among these are marine turtles, particularly the hawksbill; iguanas—brilliant green lizards; and several species of snakes. The snakes include the Cuban boa, which grows up to 13 feet

The Cuban iguana

(4 m) long. This nonvenomous reptile kills its prey, small mammals such as rats and mice, by squeezing them to death.

Smaller animal life is plentiful, with frogs, toads, and many species of mollusks and snails, including the beautifully colored Polymita snail. This snail lives in trees and is sensitive to climate conditions, so it is restricted to the eastern end of the island where its brilliant, variegated colors are famous.

The World's Smallest

When it comes to the smallest, Cuban wildlife has a place in *The Guinness Book of World Records*. The

world's smallest bird, the Cuban bee hummingbird, is found only on this island. It is about the size of a bumblebee, and grows only 2 inches (5 cm) long. When flying, it is often mistaken for a tropical insect. It is known locally as a zunzuncito (little zunzun) for the whirring sound of its tiny wings. These extraordinary birds can be seen in many different parts of the island, especially the Zapata Swamp and the Sierra Maestra mountains.

Cuba also boasts the world's smallest frog, the so-called banana frog—*Sminthillus limbatus*—which grows from 0.44 to 0.48 inch (1.1–1.2 cm). Another Cuban native is so small that you need good eyesight to spot it—it is the world's smallest scorpion, the *centuroides*. The largest of these is no more than 2.5 inches (6.4 cm) long.

A Bird Paradise

Many of the birds seen in Cuba are also found on other islands in the Caribbean region, but a few are unique to Cuba. These include the Cuban trogon, the Cuban parrot, the Cuban parakeet, the Cuban cuckoo, the Zapata wren, and a Zapata rail—one of a family of birds often found on swampy land. These birds have especially long toes so they can walk across the marshes, where they feed on a variety of small animals. Their olive-green feathers blend well with the marsh, so they are hard to see. Rails are known for their loud, strident calls that echo across the marshes in the twilight hours.

A Visit to Zapata Swamp

Wetlands have a special place in the world's environmental heritage. Low-lying land is often swampy, and great rivers have deltas where soil has been deposited for millions of years. These wetlands and their wildlife are endangered all over the world. Cuba is fortunate that almost 10 percent of its territory is classified as swamps and marshes.

The largest wetlands area in the Caribbean is the Zapata Swamp in Matanzas Province. The swamp is a maze of small lagoons, some tidal and some brackish with water from the rivers. The edges are fringed with palms, tall grasses, and sedges. Mangroves thrive in tidal areas. These tropical wetlands plants are also a haven for birds.

One of the great attractions is the Crocodile Farm, where as many as 10,000 Cuban crocodiles are being reared. They are grown for their meat and their leather, which has a high commercial value. The Cuban crocodile may reach a length of 9.8 feet (3 m), and is a longtime inhabitant of the swamp.

More than 900 species of fish have been recorded, including the odd-looking *manjuari* (alligator-gar),

a relic from the past. This unusual fish has a long head, grows almost 5.5 feet (2 m) long, and is covered with thick, rhomboid-shaped scales.

The Zapata Swamp has been set aside not only as a national park but also as a Special Region for Sustained Development. In these regions, human activity is carefully controlled so that the region's natural life will be available for many future generations.

Birds that arrive in Cuba as seasonal visitors include the greater, or Caribbean, flamingos. The pink plumage of these elegant migratory birds comes from the microscopic animals and plants they eat. They filter their food out of the water with their very specialized bill. Parts of the Cuban coastline have just the right conditions for their food to multiply, and thousands of flamingos may be seen in parts of the north coast, where they have become a tourist attraction.

Cays and Coral Reefs

Cuba's undersea world is fascinating. At eighteen dive sites, naturalists and eco-tourists from around the world plunge into some of the least-disturbed coral reefs on the planet. More than 500 species of fish have been recorded, among them sharks, moray eels, and barracudas. In addition to these well-known creatures of the ocean, countless others spend their lives in the coral between the living sponges and the fronds of seaweeds.

Most of the diving areas are in the four island regions. In addition to deep holes in the old limestone seabed, there are undersea caves and even wrecked ships that date from colonial times when Cuba was on the silver trade route to Europe.

The Island of Youth has many diving areas, but perhaps the most famous in all Cuba is the humorously named *Playa María la Gorda* (Fat Mary's Beach). It is at the western end of Cuba in a secluded bay sheltered by the Guanahacabibes Peninsula. The peninsula itself is a UNESCO Biosphere

Reserve because of the great diversity of its plants. Fat Mary is a legend from pirate days. The story goes that she was brought there as a hostage from South America. No one knows where she died or was buried.

A spotted moray eel surrounded by brightly colored coral

Remote Times and Revolution

CHRISTOPHER COLUMBUS WAS the first European to land in Cuba. He spent some weeks there during his first voyage to the Americas in 1492 and returned two years later. He wrote that he had "never seen anything so beautiful." But it was not until 1508 that the navigator Sebastián de Ocampo discovered Cuba was an island by sailing around it.

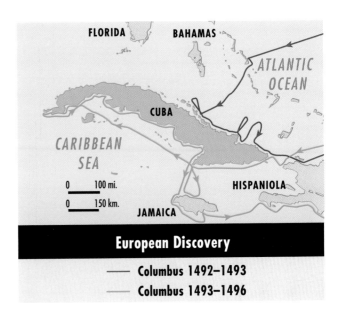

European Discovery

— Columbus 1492–1493
— Columbus 1493–1496

Cuba's original peoples were the Ciboney, who possibly date back to 3500 B.C. Later arrivals from mainland South American were the Taíno, who forced the Ciboney into the west end of the

Columbus and his ships coasting along the northern shore of Cuba

Opposite: Ancient Cuban treasures discovered in Spanish galleons, sailing ships from the fifteenth to eighteenth centuries used for war or commerce

Ancient Pictographs

Few traces remain of the early peoples, but there are more than 200 pictographs in caves on Isla de la Juventud (Island of Youth). These fascinating drawings were probably made about 3,000 years ago by the Ciboney. The drawings include circles, triangles, lines, and human and animal figures and are believed to represent some kind of calendar.

island. The Taíno took over the fertile areas, where they grew potatoes, manioc, and tobacco. They lived in villages of up to 2,000 people and knew how to make pots and weave cotton.

In 1511, the Spanish soldier and adventurer Diego Velásquez invaded eastern Cuba with a force of 300 men. At first, the Indians resisted, led by Hatuey, an Indian chief from Hispianola who had already witnessed the atrocities committed by the Spaniards. But when Hatuey was captured, the resistance crumbled. He was sentenced to burn at the stake but before dying was asked if he wanted to be baptized and become a Christian. "Are there Christians in Heaven?" Hatuey asked. When told there were many, he refused baptism, preferring to die a pagan. Cubans regard him as their first revolutionary.

The Spaniards took four months to capture eastern Cuba. Velásquez founded the island's first Spanish settlement, or *villa*, at Baracoa in 1512 and then marched west.

Diego Velásquez, the Spanish soldier who conquered Cuba

Over the next four years, Velásquez founded six other *villas*: Bayamo, Trinidad, Sancti Spíritus, *La Habana* (Havana), Puerto Príncipe (now Camagüey), and Santiago de Cuba. He made Santiago his first capital.

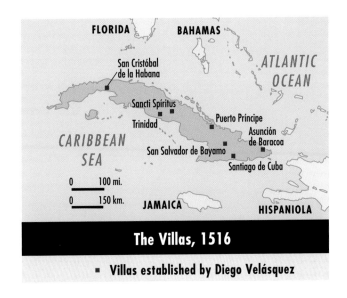

The Spanish conquerors divided the land among themselves and forced the Indians to work as slaves. Thousands of Indians died from the brutal treatment and from diseases brought by the Europeans. Indian people had no resistance to such diseases as smallpox and influenza. Marriage with the Spaniards also contributed to the gradual extinction of the Indians and the appearance of the *mestizos*, or mixed-race people.

Colonial Cuba

Early in the seventeenth century, Cuba had a population of about 20,000, with about half the people living in Havana, the island's most important city and port. Ships carrying treasure from all over Latin America gathered in Havana before sailing to Europe. Twice a year, when the fleet prepared to sail, Havana became a great commercial center as traders and craftspeople supplied the sailors with everything they needed. The great fleets attracted pirates and fortune-hunters, and the city was continually attacked and looted. To protect it, the Spaniards built forts and enlarged the harbor.

Inland, the Spaniards created vast estates for raising cattle and plantations for sugar and tobacco. Cuba's original native population was small compared to that of other colonies such as Mexico and Peru. The Indians died off quickly after the Europeans arrived, so the Spanish were faced with a shortage of workers. Soon, they began to bring black slaves from Africa to Cuba.

In the seventeenth and eighteenth centuries, tobacco was the most important crop. It was particularly in demand in Europe. Remote and uninhabited parts of Cuba were opened up as tobacco growers searched for the right soil.

Tobacco was a profitable business, and in 1717 the Spanish government angered the tobacco farmers by imposing trade restrictions that greatly reduced their profits. When the farmers protested, many of them were executed. Then, in the middle of the century, the Spanish merchants took control of all trade between Cuba and Spain. The Spaniards made huge profits and the Cubans suffered.

Toward the end of the eighteenth century, two events brought great change in Cuba. The first occurred in 1762, when the British fleet took over Havana and occupied the city for ten months. They allowed the Cubans to trade freely with other countries, and the economy boomed. Cuban merchants were furious when the Spaniards took back Havana and once again imposed trading restrictions.

The second event was the collapse of the sugar industry in nearby Haiti. In 1791, the black slaves rebelled against their white owners and both the slaves and thousands of French settlers fled to Cuba. Almost overnight, Cuba became the leading sugar producer in the Caribbean.

Thousands of African slaves worked on the plantations. They lived in appalling conditions, repressed by their owners, who feared slave revolts. In contrast, the owners lived in amazing luxury, importing works of arts, furnishings, and the latest fashions from Europe.

A sugar planter with his staff in the 1890s

Sugarcane Harvest in Cuba by Víctor Patricio de Landaluze

Latin America's first railroad, completed in 1837, connected Havana to nearby sugarcane fields. Many laborers working in miserable conditions died during its construction.

At about this time, the United States began to show an interest in buying Cuba and making it a U.S. state. Events in Europe had weakened Spain's control over its colonies and, in the early nineteenth century, many Latin American countries became independent. But Cuba remained loyal to Spain and for much of the nineteenth century it was the richest colony in the world.

Its wealth, however, depended largely on the continuing importation of black slaves into Cuba at a time when slavery was being abolished in most other countries. New slaves had to be smuggled into Cuba like contraband. The landowners brought in some Chinese laborers, but that did not solve their problem.

The Ten Years' War

Matters came to a head in 1868. Attitudes in Cuba had been changing for some time. The *peninsulares*—people who were born in Spain but living in the colonies—held most of the important administrative jobs and controlled much of the trade. They were of course still strongly pro-Spain.

But the landowners, most of whom were *creoles*— Spaniards born in the colonies—were divided. Those in western Cuba favored some kind of moderate reform, but they had large estates and the most to lose. Creoles in the east wanted nothing less than total reform and independence.

The Colonial City of Trinidad

One of the original seven *villas* of Cuba, Trinidad is on the south coast. During the eighteenth and nineteenth centuries, wealth from the nearby sugar plantations made it the finest colonial city in Cuba. Much of the old city has changed very little over the past 150 years.

At the heart of the old city lies a small square dotted with palm trees. Cobblestone streets lined with brightly colored houses run from the main square. In the center of the square is a statue of José Martí guarded by two bronze sculptures of greyhounds. Fine mansions once occupied by Trinidad's wealthiest families line the square. Some are two-storied, with wooden shutters and wrought-iron balconies. Today, the mansions are museums, complete with furniture, paintings, and family possessions of the period.

Also facing the square is the *Iglesia de la Santísima Trinidad* (Church of the Most Holy Trinity), with an altar made of eighteen different woods. One of the most treasured possessions of the church is a figure of Christ. Originally the figure was on a boat that stopped in Trinidad on its way from Spain to Mexico. Three times the boat left Trinidad for the last part of its journey to Mexico, and three times it was blown back to port by a violent storm. After the third time, the people of Trinidad decided the figure was meant to stay in their church, and they kept it.

They already faced many difficulties. Their farms were small, they could not get slaves, they were heavily taxed, and Havana was many miles away.

In 1868, the weak Spanish king was toppled in a coup. This was the moment that sugar planter Carlos Manuel de Céspedes chose to free his slaves from his small farm in eastern Cuba and set off a rebellion against Spain. A week later, he and his supporters took the town of Bayamo. Many people from eastern Cuba then joined the rebels, known as *mambises*, and became successful guerrilla fighters.

Carlos Manuel de Céspedes led an armed revolt in 1868 that began the Ten Years' War.

The leaders of the rebels were two very different men. One was General Máximo Gómez, a Dominican defector from the Spanish army. The other was Antonio Maceo, a *mulatto* (a person of mixed African and European descent) who rose from the ranks to become a general. He was known as the "Bronze Titan," and it is claimed that he fought in 900 battles, was wounded 27 times, lost his father and fourteen brothers in the war, and survived many assassination attempts.

General Máximo Gómez

For a long time, the rebels controlled eastern Cuba but were prevented by the Spaniards from invading the west, where life continued much as before, with huge sugar harvests. Some rebels favored delay anyway, hoping for help from the United States. They made only limited efforts to free the slaves, though emancipation was part of Maceo's and Gómez's strategy wherever they fought.

In 1870, the new Republican government in Spain seized the initiative by making some modest political concessions that included the first steps toward the abolition of slavery. Finally, in 1874, Gómez and Maceo were able to make some advances in the west. The war dragged on until 1878, but in the end the rebel leaders were let down by their wealthy backers who, mistrusting their army of peasants and blacks, withdrew support.

In the years following the Ten Years' War, the Spanish government did little to promote self-rule or independence in Cuba, although slavery was abolished in 1886. The last years of the war also hurt Cuba's economy—sugar

General Antonio Maceo

plantations were destroyed and their Spanish owners fled, often leaving behind huge debts. In addition to the problems it suffered because of the war, Cuba's sugar industry was affected by the development of the sugar-beet industry in Europe and the United States. After 1884, world sugar prices dropped sharply. For most of the nineteenth century, Cuba had traded more with the United States than with Spain or other countries, and in the 1880s, U.S. investors bought up many of the bankrupt Cuban plantations.

Meanwhile, Cuban exiles in the United States were plotting a return to Cuba. They were led by José Martí, whose message was that Cuba should be independent and not a part of Spain or of the United States. He spent many years arguing, talking, and lecturing to Cubans in the United States on the need for total independence and persuading them to give money to the cause. He even set up a kind of training school for revolutionaries in New York. A successful journalist and poet, Martí had a wide following, and in 1892 he started a newspaper, *Patria*, in New York.

Also in 1892, Martí and some fellow exiles founded the Cuban Revolutionary Party and enlisted the help of Gómez and Maceo. They planned their return to Cuba to coincide with mass uprisings across the island, where it was recognized generally that all political attempts to achieve Cuban reform within the Spanish system had failed. In April 1895, Martí left for Cuba from Santo Domingo with Gómez, while Maceo set out from Costa Rica, where he had a banana plantation.

The rebel *mambises* were waiting for them and, despite being greatly outnumbered by the Spaniards, they once again drove the Europeans westward. Martí died early in the campaign, "facing the sun" as he had wished in some of his immortal verses.

For two years, the United States did not intervene in the war, although its government was concerned about the welfare of U.S. citizens living in Cuba, and about the Spaniards' "ruthless treatment of the Cuban fighters they captured." Many rebels were hounded into concentration camps, where they died from disease and starvation.

Theodore Roosevelt (center), later the twenty-sixth president of the United States, with the men of the 1st Cavalry Volunteers (known as the "Rough Riders") during the Spanish-American War.

The Mystery of the *Maine*

At the beginning of 1898, the U.S. government sent the warship U.S.S. *Maine* to the Bay of Havana on the pretext of helping American nationals on the island. One month later, the ship mysteriously exploded, killing 260 crewmen. Only 88 men survived. There were many conspiracy theories, with the Spaniards, Cubans, and Americans all under suspicion. At one time, the explosion was thought to have been caused by a mine, but that theory was dashed when the wreckage was raised

and evidence showed that the explosion originated inside the ship, not outside of it. The most likely cause appears to be that the ship's boilers blew up, but the mystery has never been resolved.

At the time, however, the United States firmly believed that Spain was to blame and immediately declared war. The cry went up "Remember the Maine! The hell with Spain!" The Americans wanted to go it alone, using the Cuban rebel forces only if they had to. The 6,000-man U.S. Army focused on Santiago, in the east, where there was a large Spanish army garrison and fleet and some 700 Spanish soldiers were defending San Juan Hill. The Spaniards held off the Americans for a day before conceding defeat. Future U.S. President Teddy Roosevelt led his "Rough Riders" in a charge up Kettle Hill to victory. The largely black and mulatto Cuban army was excluded from the victory celebrations, and the U.S. flag—not the Cuban flag—was raised at the surrender ceremony.

Independence

In 1898, the U.S. Army joined the fight and defeated Spain in what became known as the Spanish-American War. A U.S. military government ruled Cuba from 1899 to 1902, when Cuba became a republic. Cuba had to agree to certain U.S. conditions before the Americans left. These included the detested Platt Amendment, which gave the United States the right to intervene in Cuban affairs at any time and to lease land on which to build naval bases. In 1903, the United States got a lease on Guantánamo Bay and built a naval base there.

Independent Cuba's first president was Tomás Estrada Palma. Opposition to his policies, however, led in 1906 to a civil-military government headed by Charles E. Magoon of the United States. The Americans left again in 1909, but U.S. investors retained control over large parts of the Cuban economy, especially the sugar industry, and the U.S. government continued to keep a close eye on affairs in Cuba. By the 1920s, U.S. companies owned two-thirds of Cuba's farmland and most of its mines.

Little was done to help the Cuban people, who were mostly poor and desperately in need of jobs, education, and a decent standard of living. In 1912, the blacks, at that time the most downtrodden segment of Cuban society, revolted. They had fought bravely for independence alongside whites and other

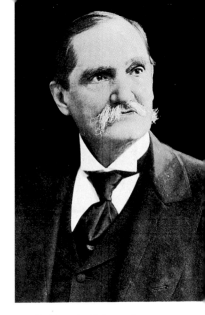

Tomás Estrada Palma, the first president of Cuba

A view of the Plaza de Aruas in Havana, April 1912

Cubans, but their efforts were never recognized. Now they set about forming their own political party. When that was banned, they rebelled with strikes and demonstrations throughout the island. President José Miguel Gómez ordered government troops to quell the riots, and some 3,000 Afro-Cubans died in the massacres that followed. The U.S. government, too, was concerned and landed a troop of U.S. Marines in the east, ostensibly to protect American sugar interests.

Gerardo Machado, politician and liberal party leader, who was president of Cuba from 1925–1933

Between 1913 and 1933, Cuba had three presidents. Their governments were marked by corruption and fraud, and each president left office a wealthy man. Mario García Menocal, a Conservative who took office in 1913, was a businessman who ran a sugar mill. He was closely identified with the United States and at first was greatly respected. But he changed the Constitution so that he could run for a second term, and he almost certainly deprived the Liberals of victory with a rigged election. He asked the United States to keep its troops in Cuba, and some 2,500 marines remained until 1923.

The Liberals were victorious when Gerardo Machado was elected in 1925. Much was expected of this amiable businessman who promised many reforms but, once in power, he too became a ruthless, tyrannical dictator. From the beginning, his regime was corrupt, siphoning off millions of dollars on loans and business contracts. He kept the support of the army with threats and bribes, had his enemies killed or imprisoned, and censored the press. The U.S. government was deceived by his charm for a long time, even when he extended his term of office and then broke a promise not to have himself reelected president.

During Machado's second term, serious protests among the student community, a failed Conservative coup, and the obvious near-bankruptcy of the country led the U.S. government to think differently. Many Cubans wanted the United States to intervene. Finally, a general strike brought matters to a head. The United States attempted to mediate a solution, but once Machado lost the Cuban army's support, he was doomed. Riots broke out in Havana and other cities, and Machado fled to the Bahamas.

The new government created to succeed him in 1933 was unable to stop the riots. In the same year, a revolt by the military, led by Colonel Fulgencio Batista, led to the formation of a new revolutionary government. With reservations, the U.S. government accepted the situation and refused to intervene. Batista was not a member of the revolutionary government. Instead he became chief of the army. A mulatto from a lowly background, Batista had moved swiftly through the ranks to this very powerful position. He was the true dictator of Cuba. By May 1934, relations with the United States had improved under President Franklin Delano Roosevelt. The hated Platt Amendment was finally repealed, and the lease on Guantánamo Bay was extended for ninety-nine years.

The Batista Regime

In 1940, a new Constitution set out political rights and social legislation, such as a minimum wage, pensions, an eight-hour workday and forty-four-hour workweek, accident compensation, and insurance. Presidential elections were also held. Batista duly resigned as chief of the army and was elected president. When he took office, Batista had the support of all Cubans, rich and poor alike. His main opposition came from resentful army comrades. Economic aid was forthcoming from the United States after Cuba declared against Japan, Germany, and Italy in World War II (1939–1945). Cuba's declaration meant that the United States could use Cuban airfields and other facilities if needed.

Fulgencio Batista, former president of Cuba, at a press interview in 1942

The war years were relatively prosperous for Cuba and, entering democratic elections in 1944, Batista could well expect that his chosen candidate would win. However, he did not win, and Cuba's next two governments proved to be corrupt and inefficient. Batista himself left office a wealthy man.

After the war, Cuba became a playground for rich Americans attracted by the sunshine, drugs, music, easy living, prostitution, casinos, and luxury hotels. The Mafia controlled much of this business. It was a period of extreme decadence and corruption, carried on against a background of ever-increasing poverty for the majority of the Cuban people. In material terms, Cuba was one of the wealthiest nations in Latin America, but there was high unemployment, and Cubans, particularly in rural areas, lived in dreadful poverty with few medical facilities or schools.

Batista seized power again in 1952 with a military coup. His dictatorial government was harsh and cruel. He abolished the Constitution and dissolved Congress, thus canceling elections in which the young lawyer Fidel Castro might well have been elected to the House of Representatives.

On July 26, 1953, now a revered date in the history of the Revolution, Fidel Castro and 125 anti-Batista revolutionaries staged an attack on the Moncada army barracks in Santiago. It was a dismal failure. Some of the rebels died and many, including Castro, were taken prisoner. But that attack was the beginning of the Cuban Revolution and the monumental changes that were to come.

Castro was taken prisoner and brought to trial. He used the trial to make his famous speech "History Will Absolve Me," in which he denounced Batista and appealed for reforms that could change the lives of ordinary Cubans. Everyone, he said, should receive education, and the large plantations should be broken up so that every family had its own piece of land.

Castro was sentenced to fifteen years' imprisonment and sent to the Isle of Pines (now known as the Island of Youth). In 1954, a general election was held in which Batista was returned to power unopposed. The new Congress assembled early the following year. In February 1955, Batista was declared president for another term. Just two months later he felt in a strong enough position to announce an amnesty of political prisoners, which included Fidel Castro, Castro's brother Raúl, and other rebels.

Revolution

Castro and his followers went to Mexico, leaving behind a schoolteacher named Frank País to organize the underground resistance of the newly formed 26th of July Movement. In Mexico, Castro met Ernesto "Che" Guevara of Argentina, who joined the rebels and helped plan their return to Cuba.

Fidel Castro with his revolutionaries at a secret base near Cuba's coast in 1957

Late in 1956, in a secondhand yacht called the *Granma*, eighty-two guerrillas wearing "26th of July" armbands landed on the eastern coast of Cuba. But word of their coming had preceded them, and they were met by Batista's forces. Many were captured, but about a dozen, including Fidel, Raúl, and Che, escaped into the Sierra Maestra.

They began to create the Rebel Army, enlisting support among local villagers and spreading their message by radio. News of their campaign reached the United States, where they received good press. They gained the support of other anti-Batista groups and movements in Cuba, and followers from towns and villages across Cuba helped swell their numbers. During 1957, guerrilla attacks on army barracks and other institutions increased, with bombs, strikes, and assassinations—including one unsuccessful attempt on Batista by the students. Meanwhile, the number of rebels increased. By 1958, the Rebel Army had about 50,000 fighters and Cuba was in a state of civil war.

A general strike in April 1958 almost toppled Batista. The following month, he sent his army into the Sierra Maestra to eliminate the rebels. By August, it was clear that the army had failed. In fact, the rebels had captured great quantities of arms from the soldiers.

Presidential elections held in November were won by Batista's candidate, but fewer than a third of the people voted. It seemed unlikely that the new president would ever be inaugurated. Time was running out for Batista. His troops suffered further severe defeats in November and December.

Che Guevara

Ernesto "Che" Guevara was born in Argentina in 1928 of left-wing, middle-class parents. He qualified as a doctor before setting off on a hitch-hiking trip around Latin America, inspired by socialist ideals to help the poor and deprived.

He first joined the Cuban rebels in Mexico as a doctor but soon was fighting alongside them. He became a military commander in the Rebel Army. Although injured twice, he survived to play an important part in the new revolutionary government. He was a hero to young radical groups across the world for his ideals and his brilliant intellect.

In 1965, Guevara left Cuba. His reasons are unclear, but his passion for revolution and helping the poor was apparently greater than his enthusiasm for government responsibilities. In 1961, he had taken charge of Cuba's Ministry of Industry, with responsibility for some 287 industries and a workforce of 150,000. The challenge was to make existing industry more productive, to centralize industry, and to intro-

duce new industries. This proved to be an almost impossible task, and Cuba turned to the Soviet Union and other Communist countries for technical and financial help.

Guevara then headed off for Bolivia, where he hoped to create another revolution among the peasants of the Andes. In 1967, he was captured by the Bolivian military with the help of the U.S. Central Intelligence Agency (CIA) and was executed. Over thirty years later, his remains were returned to Cuba and buried with military honors in Santa Clara (below).

Che's memory lives on in posters, monuments, murals, books, and films. In Cuba, he is a hero and a martyr, and even now Cuban schoolchildren begin their day with the slogan, "Pioneers of communism, we shall be like Che."

Fidel Castro, surrounded by his mountain rebels, speaks in front of the Palacio Municipal of Santa Clara in early 1959 before his march to Havana.

Shortly after midnight on January 1, 1959, Batista boarded a plane with some of his officials and left Cuba. On New Year's Day, Che Guevara and Camilo Cienfuegos took over Havana's military post. Hours later, at the other end of the island, Fidel Castro received a hero's welcome in Santiago and gave his first victory speech. From there, he and some of his men drove to Havana, greeted by cheering crowds along the route.

The Revolutionary Government

By the end of 1959, many changes had taken place and the direction in which Cuba was heading became clearer. The island would be governed by a Council of Ministers, with Fidel Castro as prime minister and his brother Raúl as deputy. War trials were held within months of victory, followed by imprisonment or execution by firing squad. The trials were directed mainly against Batista's army and supporters. And although Fidel Castro had yet to make his leanings toward communism clear, some of his own supporters expressed their fears. They too were imprisoned. Even Camilio Cienfuegos, the revolutionary leader who was almost as popular as Castro himself, disappeared in a mysterious plane crash.

Many people were singled out and, for one reason or another, accused by Castro of being counterrevolutionary. Most received long prison sentences; some were shot. Newspapers

A crowd of cheering Cuban children awaits future resettlement at a refugee camp south of Miami.

were censored as the free press began to disappear. All private schools were nationalized. The 1940 Constitution was suspended and elections were postponed for eighteen months.

Cuba's relations with the United States deteriorated quickly as reform led to the nationalization of American-owned sugar plantations and cattle ranches. At the same time, Cuba became more friendly with the Soviet Union and China.

Hundreds of thousands of Cubans who did not like the left-wing trend fled Cuba. Their properties were confiscated by the government. These people included wealthy landowners and businessmen, scientists, engineers, and technicians, teachers and doctors, artists and writers, and many others who felt their lives were at risk. In Operation Peter Pan, some 15,000 children traveled alone to the United States because of fears that the government would take them away from their parents. Most priests and nuns were expelled from the country. Most of the exiles settled in Florida, which became the center of a counterrevolutionary anti-Castro campaign. Opponents to the regime flew planes over Cuba, dropping small bombs and leaflets denouncing Castro.

During 1960, Cuba strengthened its ties with the Soviet Union. In June, when U.S.-owned oil refineries on the island refused to handle Soviet oil, Cuba nationalized the companies. In response, the U.S. government cut back on the amount of sugar it bought from Cuba. The Soviet Union then stepped in and offered to take the surplus. Within a few months, Cuba nationalized most of the remaining U.S. companies, and the United States retaliated by forbidding

The Bay of Pigs Invasion

For some time, the United States had been seeking ways to get rid of Castro, allegedly including use of an "exploding cigar" and poison. The CIA began to work with Cuban exiles, planning an invasion of Cuba. However, an early attempt to destroy Cuba's air force not only failed, but also gave Castro warning of the coming attack. When a force of some 1,300 Cuban exiles began to land at the Bay of Pigs in April 1961, Castro was waiting in person with some 20,000 troops. He also ordered his remaining air force to bomb the U.S. supply ships.

There was great confusion. Some exiles were able to land while others could not. Gradually it became clear that help was not forthcoming from the U.S. gov-ernment and Castro's troops were closing in on the exiles. Some exiles managed to get away in small boats but the great majority—1,180 of the 1,297 who had landed—were taken prisoner.

U.S. companies to trade with Cuba. In January 1961, the United States ended diplomatic relations with Cuba.

In April 1961, Castro and his troops defeated a group of exiles attempting to invade Cuba at the Bay of Pigs. Castro chose this moment to announce that the Revolution was fundamentally socialist, and that he was a Marxist-Leninist. Some academics believe he was pressured into this position to ensure continued support from the Soviet Union and China. To get support from ordinary Cubans, he created Committees for the Defense of the Revolution and organizations including the Union of Young Communists and the Federation of Cuban Women. Anyone who did not join one of these organizations was suspected of being antirevolutionary.

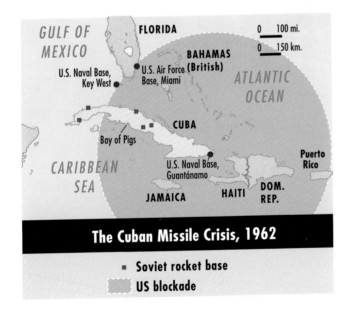

The Cuban Missile Crisis, 1962

- ■ Soviet rocket base
- ▨ US blockade

The Cuban Missile Crisis

Cuba received more than economic, technical, and financial support from the Soviet Union. It also received weapons. In October 1962, the United States learned that Cuba had a number of long-range missiles with nuclear warheads capable of targeting U.S. cities. This led to a confrontation that threatened the world with nuclear war. President John F. Kennedy ordered a naval blockade to prevent any further shipments arriving from the Soviet Union, and he demanded that all missiles and missile bases be removed from Cuba. For several days, the world held its breath. Finally, the Soviets agreed, but only after the United States agreed not to invade Cuba.

The Communist Regime

CUBA DREW UP A NEW CONSTITUTION IN 1976, THE first since the 1959 Revolution. The Constitution declares that the Republic of Cuba is a socialist and independent state that carries out the will of the working people and guarantees them work, medical care, education, food, clothing, and housing. It also recognizes the right of small farmers to own and work their land.

Opposite: **The Capitol in Havana displaying the Cuban flag**

According to the Constitution, the National Assembly of People's Power is the "supreme organ of state power." It is a one-chamber parliament with the power to pass, amend, and repeal laws. It meets twice a year. Deputies—representatives to the National Assemby—must be over the age of eighteen and are elected every five years. All Cubans over the age of sixteen, except the mentally ill or criminal, can vote, although 1993 was the first time Cubans were allowed a direct secret vote. The 1998 National Assembly had 601 members.

The National Assembly elects thirty-one members to form the Council of State. The president of the Council of State is also the head of state and government. Five vice presidents and a secretary are elected from the thirty-one members. The Council of State represents the National Assembly when the Assembly is not in session.

The Council of Ministers is Cuba's top executive and administrative body. It is appointed by the National Assembly on the advice of the head of state and government. The council is

Fidel Castro

Fidel Castro Ruz was born in 1926 to a Spanish farmer and his housekeeper, whom his father later married. Fidel grew up surrounded by a large family. They were wealthy by local standards, and his father employed many people on the farm. Fidel went to a Roman Catholic school, and later to a Jesuit college. He graduated from the University of Havana with a law degree and practiced law for a short time. At the university, he was known for his political views and his ability to stir up student protests. He was also a talented athlete, considered good enough to play professional baseball in the United States.

In 1948, he married a distant relative of Batista's. The Castros had a son in 1949, and five years later they divorced.

Castro decided on a career in politics, but his attempt to enter Congress was foiled when Batista canceled elections in 1952. At that time, Castro decided that revolution by violence and insurrection was the only answer to Cuba's problems. Since the Revolution of 1959, he has been the country's prime minister, and since 1976, its president, although he was not elected by universal vote. He is the longest-serving head of state in the world today.

Despite the ups and downs, Castro remains firmly in control and is still popular. Officially, he is commander in chief of the armed forces, first secretary of the Central Committee of the Cuban Communist Party, and president of the Councils of State and Ministers. Unofficially, he is *el presidente, el comandante, el jefe,* or just *Fidel.* He has many opponents, although most have been silenced. Nearly a million Cubans have

gone into exile, and hundreds of others are political prisoners in Cuba.

The Cuban leader is now over seventy years old and apparently is in good health. He still delivers the lengthy speeches for which he is renowned. Without notes or interruption, he spoke for seven and a half hours at the Fifth Congress of the Communist Party in October 1997. But many people wonder what will happen after his death. His charisma holds the people together, and in many ways, he *is* "The Revolution." He has named his brother Raúl (right) as his successor, but the two are close in age and there is no guarantee that Raúl will outlive Fidel. It may be significant that Fidel has begun to appoint younger men to top jobs.

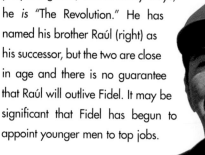

chaired by the head of state and government and the first vice president and includes other vice presidents, a secretary, ministers, and administrators of national agencies. It implements agreements reached by the National Assembly, enforces laws, plans development, directs Cuba's foreign policy, and controls national security.

The National Assembly also appoints the president, vice president, and other judges of the People's Supreme Court, which is the highest court in Cuba. Judges are independent but must inform the people of their activities at least once a year.

NATIONAL GOVERNMENT OF CUBA

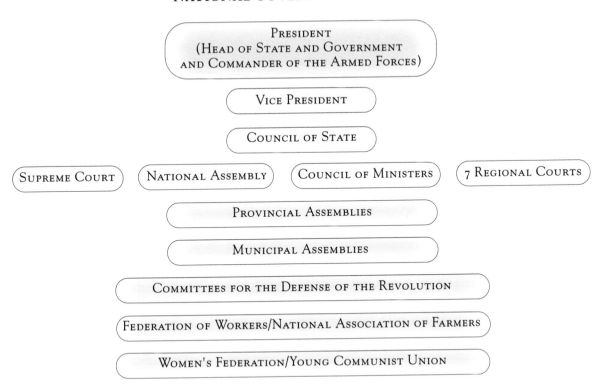

The Communist Party

The real power in Cuba lies with the *Partido Comunista de Cuba* (PCC), or Communist Party, described in the Constitution as "the highest leading force of society and the State." It is the only political party allowed in Cuba and selects its members from outstanding workers or other deserving people. Membership stands at about 600,000. The vast majority of National Assembly delegates are party members.

The party's highest authority is Congress, which meets approximately every five years. Congress elects a Central Committee, made up of some 225 members, which supervises the party's work. A Politburo of about twenty-five people is elected by the Central Committee to direct policy. It is headed by Fidel Castro as first secretary and his brother Raúl as second secretary.

The interior of the Capitol, Havana

The party has municipal committees in each of the country's provinces and municipalities, and it penetrates every corner of Cuban life through its grassroots committees. These committees are found in workplaces, student bodies, military units, and residential areas. In some instances, party committees oversee the work of several grassroots organizations.

Scenic view of the Delta
Hotel in Santiago de Cuba

Local Government

Cuba is divided into fourteen provinces, which are further divided into 169 municipalities. From west to east, the provinces are Pinar del Río, La Habana, Ciudad de la Habana, Matanzas, Villa Clara, Cienfuegos, Sancti Spíritus, Ciego de Avila, Camagüey, Las Tunas, Holguín, Granma, Santiago de Cuba, and Guantánamo. Isla de la Juventud (Isle of Youth) is not a part of any province and is responsible directly to the central government.

Each province and municipality has its own assembly, which passes local laws and appoints administrators. The municipal assemblies elect the delegates to the provincial assembly. Some provincial delegates also become deputies to the National Assembly.

Provinces

The National Flag and Emblem

The Cuban flag was raised for the first time in 1850 in the city of Cárdenas by a group of anti-Spanish revolutionaries. It was designed by writer, poet, and artist Miguel Teurbe Tolón and has three blue stripes representing the departments into which the island was divided at that time. Two white stripes represent the purity of the ideals of independence. The three equal sides of the triangle on the left stand for equality, liberty, and fraternity, and its color—red—stands for the blood shed in the battle for independence. A white star at the center of the triangle symbolizes liberty.

Newspapers are displayed in windows because of a shortage of newsprint and ink.

Many local groups are involved in the selection and nomination of delegates, including representatives of youth, workers, farmers, revolutionary, and women's organizations. Though these groups are not officially controlled by the Communist Party, they are closely linked to it. Their main object is to secure allegiance to the socialist state.

Collapse of the Soviet Union

Since the 1960s, the revolutionary government has had great success with its education and health programs. It has also been very active in supporting other revolutionaries around the world, particularly in Africa and Nicaragua. But relations

with the United States have been strained, and Cuba relied heavily on the former Soviet Union for economic aid and good trade deals. Cuba's own economy has suffered from bad management and a lack of trained people and technical skills.

In the late 1980s and early 1990s, the collapse of communism in Eastern Europe and the Soviet Union was a disaster for Cuba. There was no more financial aid or good trade deals, and thousands of Soviet technicians and military advisors were withdrawn, along with the Soviet troops. At the same time, the United States tightened its trade embargo by passing the Helms-Burton Act in 1996, which seeks to impose sanctions on countries trading with or investing in Cuba. Votes in the United Nations have constantly opposed the United States in this matter, and some countries, such as Canada and Mexico, have expressed very strong objections to the act.

Rations of bread are distributed on the streets in Santiago de Cuba.

Since 1990, the Cuban people have seen hard times. Castro introduced a "Special Period in Peacetime," which calls for strict rationing of food and other goods. By 1994, things were so bad that thousands of people tried to leave the island. They were tired of the continual food shortages, unemployment, and restrictions. Since then, the Cuban government has recognized that, despite its belief in communism, some economic changes are necessary if the country is to survive.

National Security and Defense

For a time after the Revolution, the Cuban government considered abolishing the armed forces. But its difficult relations with the United States were sufficient to justify a buildup of the military, and today Cuba has one of the largest and best-equipped armies in Latin America. In addition to armed forces numbering over 53,000, the nation has a large number of paramilitary forces, which include State Security troops, border guards, a civil defense, and a Youth Labor Army.

Young Cuban men between sixteen and fifty years old are drafted into the army for two years, unless they choose to work on the land. The army, which also includes a high number of women, does many nonmilitary jobs such as sugarcane harvesting and farmwork.

Cuba is a police state, and the Ministry of the Interior is responsible for preserving law and order. The police and the State Security Department rely heavily on ordinary Cubans to help them. The Committees for the Defense of the Revolution, founded in 1960, are a network of civilian spies that keep watch on the people in their neighborhoods.

The police check everyone's papers because travel to Havana is restricted.

More recently, Rapid Response Brigades were created in 1991 as a result of the worsening conditions that followed the withdrawal of the Soviet Union. Their job is to identify dissenters—anyone who is against the Castro regime—and if necessary deal with them. The brigades, which include members of the security forces, have gained a reputation for intimidation and brutality.

Despite Cuban hostility, the United States maintains a base at Guantánamo Bay, with some 3,000 troops and their families. The base includes a golf course, sporting facilities, cinemas, and supermarkets, but it is surrounded by trenches, land mines, security fences, and watchtowers. Many thousands of Cubans who tried to flee in 1994 were captured and forced to stay at the Guantánamo base until their future was resolved.

The National Anthem

Cuba's national anthem was composed by Pedro Figueredo, a lawyer and musician of the city of Bayamo, in eastern Cuba. He wrote the music in 1867, a year before the Ten Years' War began. Figueredo was later taken prisoner and shot by the Spaniards.

La Bayamesa (The Bayamo Song) became the national anthem in 1902. Its lyrics begin:

Al combate corred bayameses, que la patria os contempla orgullosa!
No temáis una muerte gloriosa, que morir por la patria es vivir.
En cadenas vivir, es vivir en afrenta y oprobio sumido,
Del clarín escuchad el sonido, A las armas valientes, corred!

(English translation)
Run to the fight Bayameses, for the fatherland is watching you proudly!
Do not fear a glorious death, for to die for the fatherland is to live.
To live in chains is to live in dishonor and ignominy,
From the clarion hear the sound, To the weapons, valiant warriors, run!

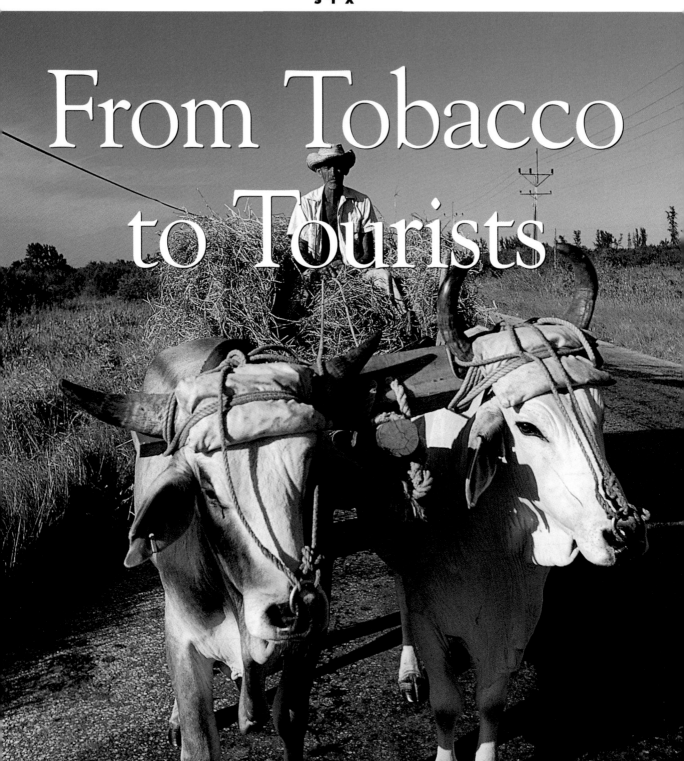

From Tobacco to Tourists

CUBA COULD BE THE WEALTHIEST ISLAND IN THE Caribbean. It has good fertile land, some minerals, and with its sunshine, its beautiful white beaches, and its elegant palm trees, the nation has the potential for a great tourist industry too. It also has a labor force that is young, healthy, and well educated.

Opposite: **A farmer drives a bullock cart on the Isla de la Juventud.**

A beach at Varadero

However, history and politics have dictated otherwise for the time being. The island was first exploited by the Spaniards, who introduced sugarcane and cattle and encouraged the growing of tobacco. Then, in the nineteenth and twentieth centuries, Americans bought up land cheaply, particularly sugar plantations, and most of the profits went back to America.

Following the 1959 Revolution, the government nationalized almost everything, thereby losing foreign investment and skills. The economic proposals of the revolutionary government were badly managed and did not work. Many professional people, including highly educated engineers and technicians, left Cuba at the time of the Revolution.

More recently, the political influence of the Soviet Union and its extensive financial aid limited Cuba to the production of sugar and other agricultural goods. It had little chance of developing the rest of its economy. As long as Cuba received oil from the Soviet Union in return for sugar, and was able to import consumer goods, everything was fine.

The Trade Embargo

The trade embargo placed on Cuba by the United States in 1962 and reinforced in the 1990s has made it difficult for the Cubans to earn hard currency—U.S. dollars. They need dollars to pay for imports necessary to run their own industries. Ironically, the island was kept afloat for a while by huge amounts of dollars sent by Cubans-in-exile to their families in Cuba. This practice was stopped by the U.S. government in 1994.

In February 1996, Cuban pilots shot down two U.S. light aircraft piloted by Cuban-American exiles, killing the four crew members. An international inquiry confirmed that the exiles were flying over international waters, and as a result President Bill Clinton signed the Helms-Burton bill, officially called the Cuban Liberty and Solidarity Act. This legislation seeks to impose sanctions on any country that trades or invests in Cuba. It has been criticized by several countries, including Canada, Mexico, and Italy, all of which have business interests on the island. In 1998, after the visit of Pope John Paul II, sanctions were eased. The United States allowed shipments of medical and other supplies to reach the island, and Cuban-American families were again allowed to send dollars to Cuba.

What Cuba Grows, Makes, and Mines

Agriculture (1996)

Sugarcane	40,000,000 metric tons
Potatoes	364,000 metric tons
Oranges and tangerines	291,000 metric tons
Grapefruit	261,000 metric tons

Manufacturing (1990) *(in U.S. dollars)*

Tobacco products	$2,629,000,000
Food products	$1,003,000,000
Beverages	$358,000,000

Mining (1996)

Nickel	50,000 metric tons
Chromite	30,000 metric tons

A lack of animal feed has reduced the size of the herds in Cuba.

Agriculture

Cuba's economy has always been based on agriculture. About 80 percent of the land is cultivated, and more than 70 percent is owned by the state. After the Revolution, small farmers were allowed to keep farms of fewer than 166 acres (67 hectares).

After sugar, the principal crops are tobacco, coffee, rice, corn, cassava, sweet potatoes, beans, and tropical fruit, such as citrus fruits, bananas, and pineapples. The livestock industry consists mainly of cattle and pigs, but the difficulty in getting animal feed since 1990 has reduced the size of the herds. Even in the countryside, milk and eggs are rationed and scarce.

Tobacco

Many of the small private farms are in the western province of Pinar del Río, where the soil is well suited to tobacco, producing cigars for which Cuba is famous. The care needed to grow tobacco plants is best provided by small farmers. The growing season begins in October or November, when the tiny seeds are sown in seedbeds. The seedlings are then transferred into the fields and planted by hand.

Tobacco farmers spend days and nights in the fields during the ninety-day growing season, pulling weeds and ridding the plants of any pests. When the plants are ready for harvesting, their lower leaves are picked first, gradually working up to the upper leaves, which have the most flavor. The leaves are then sorted and dried in a barn for up to forty-five days before being sent away for grading and processing.

A farmer at work in tobacco fields of the Viñales Valley

Traditionally, sugarcane was cut by hand using a machete, but in the 1970s many plantations were mechanized. The machinery, which came from the Soviet Union and Eastern Europe, was not the most up to date and did not always function properly, but it helped increase production. With mechanization, the average yearly harvest until the 1990s was about 7 million tons. During the 1990s, it dropped to 4 million tons. Spare parts to keep the machinery going are almost nonexistent, while fuel is both expensive and in very short

Sugarcane is again being cut by hand.

supply. So, once again, the cane is being cut by hand. Sugar is so important to Cuba's economy—in 1992 it accounted for almost two-thirds of foreign earnings—that workers are brought from the cities to help with the harvest.

In 1996, Cuba obtained some foreign financing for the sugar industry and the harvest improved to 4.5 million tons. But it is dangerous for any country to rely on a single product. Other factors that can affect the sugar industry are hurricanes and drought, either of which can devastate a harvest. Also beyond Cuba's control are world sugar prices, which give a poor return on sugar exports when they are low.

Fishing

Fishing is also an important industry in Cuba. Since the Revolution, the government has increased the size of the fishing fleet many times over and has organized fishing cooperatives. The principal catches are tuna and hake from international waters, and shrimp, lobster, mackerel, and red snapper near the coast. Havana is the main fishing port.

Mining and Industry

Cuba's natural resources include nickel, copper, iron, cobalt, chromite, tungsten, and manganese. There are significant reserves of oil along the north coast, and large deposits of limestone throughout the island are used to make cement and fertilizer. All are owned by the government.

Cuba has one of the world's largest reserves of nickel and is now the world's fourth-largest producer. Nickel-processing

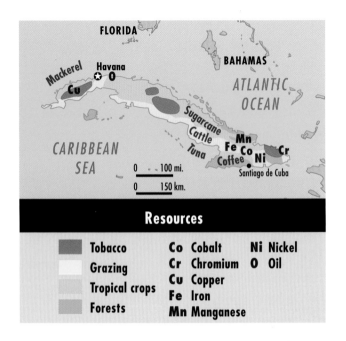

Resources

■ Tobacco	**Co** Cobalt **Ni** Nickel
□ Grazing	**Cr** Chromium **O** Oil
■ Tropical crops	**Cu** Copper
■ Forests	**Fe** Iron
	Mn Manganese

plants were originally built by North Americans, but all were nationalized when Castro took power. After nationalization, Soviet technicians took over. Recently Canadian companies have become involved, and once again production levels are high.

For many years, Cuba relied on the Soviet Union for manufactured goods and did little to develop its own manufacturing capability. Most manufacturing industries in Cuba are based on agricultural products, such as sugar, dairy products, and flour, but others include chemicals, paper, cement, and some timber. Textiles and clothing are also produced but are often in short supply because cotton has to be imported.

The bare shelves of a pharmacy in Havana show the effects of the economic embargo.

Cigars are made in factories across the island. In long rooms, seated at wooden benches one behind the other, men and women hand-roll cigars. Traditionally, in some factories one individual reads aloud to the workers—from the daily paper in the morning, and from a piece of literature in the afternoon. A good worker makes about ninety cigars a day.

A success story in Cuba and one that has proved profitable is biotechnology. After the Revolution, Cuba gained a worldwide reputation for the high quality and standards of its health service. But the U.S. trade embargo made it difficult to import medicines from overseas, and since 1981 the Cuban government has invested millions of dollars in its pharmaceutical and medical equipment industries. Cuba now sells more than 200 medical products, mainly to other developing countries. Some Western governments and scientists are also interested in Cuban-produced vaccines against diseases such as hepatitis B and meningitis.

Weights and Measures

Cuba officially uses the metric system, but U.S. and old Spanish systems are also used. For example, sugar sacks are weighed in pounds, with 1 sack equaling 329.59 pounds (149.49 kg). Land is measured in *caballerías*, with 1 *caballería* equaling 33 acres (13.4 ha).

The Special Period

The collapse of the Soviet Union was devastating for Cuba. No longer was there financial or technical support, and gone were the subsidized supplies of oil, raw materials, and consumer goods along with Cuba's major export markets. Between 1989 and 1991, Cuban exports to the Soviet Union and the other Communist countries fell from U.S.$8.1 billion to U.S.$3.6 billion.

In 1990, the government introduced the "Special Period in Peacetime." Cubans have had ration books since 1962, but

Food rationing impacts country-dwellers less because they are able to grow vegetables and own a few farm animals.

Trucks used as group taxis become crowded quickly because public transportation has dwindled.

never before had things been so bad. Just about every type of food and many household products were in short supply or just impossible to get. Everyone was expected to do their best, to make sacrifices, and somehow to get by. There were, and still are, long lines to buy bread, eggs, and milk, and meat is a luxury. The food a family can buy with the ration books is barely enough to keep them alive. In rural areas, things are a little better because people can grow their own vegetables and keep a few animals.

Without oil, there is virtually no transport. In towns, bicycles have taken over from motorized vehicles, and in the countryside ox-drawn plows and horses and carts were pressed back into service. Public transportation has dwindled to almost nothing. A train still connects Havana to Santiago, and there are flights between all major towns, but there are few long-haul buses or trucks. Getting produce to the markets is a real problem.

Cost of Living

The average wage in Cuba is about U.S.$16 per month, the equivalent of 380 ordinary pesos. The chart below shows rations and their prices from January to March 1998. (Costs are per person per month unless indicated otherwise.)

	Total cost in pesos/centavos
1 bread roll per day	.05
6 pounds (2.7 kg) rice	1.44
20 ounces (567 g) beans	.30
3 pounds (1.4 kg) white sugar	.54
3 pounds (1.4 kg) brown sugar	.24
3/4 pound (0.3 kg) salt	.08
1 bar of toilet soap every 2–3 months	.25
1 bar of washing soap every 2–3 months	.20
1 tube of toothpaste per family every 2 months	.65
6 eggs	.18
1 pound (0.4 kg) chicken	.70
3/4 pound (0.3 kg) soy mince meat twice in 3 months	.45
1/2 pound (0.2 kg) meat paste per person twice in 3 months	.50
2 ounces (56 g) coffee every 15 days	.12
6 pounds (2.7 kg) potatoes	.30
1 bottle of liquid detergent per family every 2 months	3.60
1 pound (0.4 kg) *jurel* (fish)	.35
1/2 pound (0.2 kg) cooking oil from donations received— 5 cents must be paid to support its transportation	

Children

14 jars preserves monthly from birth to 3 years	3.50 (total cost)
1 liter fresh milk daily from birth to 7 years	.25
2 bags soy yogurt monthly from 7 to 13 years	.25 each

Recent Developments

At the Fourth Congress of the Communist Party in 1993, Fidel Castro vowed that Cuba would survive the collapse of the Soviet Union and would remain a Communist state. However, he has had to make some changes of a more capitalist nature.

In 1993, the government decreed that Cubans would be allowed to start private businesses and be self-employed in about 100 specific trades. People had to get licenses, but within a short time barbers, shoe repairers, manicurists, and

Cuban women visit a streetside beautician.

others were hard at work—often on sidewalks. Small restaurants were also authorized, provided they were in private homes and seated no more than twelve people at a time. They were also restricted in the types of food they could serve so that they did not compete with state restaurants.

Another concession was to set up markets where farmers could sell fresh produce without prices being fixed. Some manufactured goods were sold on the same basis.

The Cuban government now welcomes foreign involvement. Despite the U.S. embargo, some overseas companies—particularly from Mexico, Spain, Canada, Italy, and Panama—have invested in tourism, mining, energy, communications, and agriculture. Cuba plans to convert as many international transactions as possible from the dollar to the Euro as the European currency is phased into use.

Perhaps the most radical change was the decision to allow the U.S. dollar to become legal currency. In the past, possessing dollars could lead to a prison sentence. Now some people are paid part of their salary in dollars. Salaries are also paid in "convertible" pesos, 1 of which is equal to U.S.$1, or in "ordinary" pesos, of which about 23 are equal to U.S.$1.

Legalizing the dollar carries the danger of creating two levels of society. People with dollars can enjoy a much better lifestyle than Cubans who have only ordinary pesos. While the shelves of most shops are bare, some stores have all kinds of goods, from cornflakes to designer jeans and the latest CDs. They are known as "dollar stores" because the goods can only be purchased with dollars or "convertible" pesos.

Currency

Three types of currency are used in Cuba:

- the U.S. dollar
- the "convertible" peso (1 peso = U.S.$1)
- the ordinary peso (23 pesos to U.S.$1 in 1999, but fluctuates)

Cuba's 3-peso note carries an image of Che Guevara cutting sugarcane. Underneath are the words "forerunner of voluntary work." This is a reference to the program Guevara introduced when he was Minister of Industry to encourage all Cubans to work longer and harder—not for money, but for the good of the country and the people. Che as a cane-cutter is symbolic of Cuba's working man.

Tourism

Tourism is Cuba's great hope for the future. Already the industry is bringing in millions of dollars, and tourism is top of the list for foreign investors. While the Cuban government formerly owned and ran all the island's hotels, many are now financed and built by overseas companies. The revolutionary government that once frowned on tourism as being "elitist" and "decadent" now welcomes visitors.

The number of visitors has increased rapidly. Between 1963 and 1975, about 3,000 tourists came to Cuba each year. By 1984, the number had increased to 200,000, and in the mid 1990s, it was over 700,000. In the

Tourists enjoy the pool at a resort hotel in Marea del Portillo.

year 2000, 2 million visitors are expected. About one-fourth of the tourists come from Canada, but Cuba is also a popular destination for people from Italy, Germany, Spain, Mexico, and Argentina.

The government considers tourism a priority. It makes sure that the resorts are well supplied with energy, transport, food, and other goods, even at the expense of the Cuban people. While tourists enjoy buffet lunches or meals of selected meats, imported cheeses, salads and vegetables, fruit juices, and fresh coffee, Cubans in nearby towns wait in line for hours for their meager rations.

Of course, tourism also creates jobs in construction and in servicing the resorts. But the irony and sadness is that waiters, maids, and bellhops who are paid in dollars at tourist resorts often earn more than Cuba's highly trained doctors, teachers, and engineers in their peso-paying state jobs.

Tourists take a boat ride in Key Largo.

Cubans

THE AMERICAN INDIANS WHO LIVED IN CUBA WHEN THE Spaniards arrived had all but disappeared by the end of the sixteenth century. Now only a few traces of these early peoples remain. The name *Cuba* is said to derive from one of the tribes. Bohíos, the thatched-roofed huts built today, are similar in style to those used by the Ciboney people. Another legacy is tobacco. After Columbus's men encountered Indians "with a half burnt weed in their hands, being the herbs they are accustomed to smoke," the habit was taken up in Europe.

Between the sixteenth and nineteenth centuries, more than 500,000 black slaves arrived in Cuba. Most belonged to the Yoruba and Bantu tribes of West Africa. By the 1840s, slaves made up almost half the country's population. Most ended up on the sugar plantations, but some managed to escape. The escapees, known as *cimarrones*, fled into the forests and mountains and established communities called *palenques* where they were able to live relatively free lives. In the early twentieth century, another 250,000 blacks arrived in Cuba from Jamaica and Haiti to work on the plantations.

Opposite: **Schoolchildren pose in front of a mural of Che Guevara.**

A busy Saturday morning in Sancti Spíritus shows the many origins of Cuban people.

The white Cubans are mainly descendants of Spanish immigrants and of the French settlers who fled Haiti after the slave rebellion in 1791. Between 1900 and 1930 about 1 million workers from Spain and the Canary Islands also arrived.

The only other immigrants who arrived in large numbers were the Chinese. Some 150,000 Chinese came to work as laborers during the nineteenth century. Many returned to China when their eight-year contracts ran out, but more arrived in the twentieth century, and stayed. Many mixed marriages have led to few pure ethnic Chinese in Cuba today.

A farmer and his grandson from El Sitio near the Viñales Valley

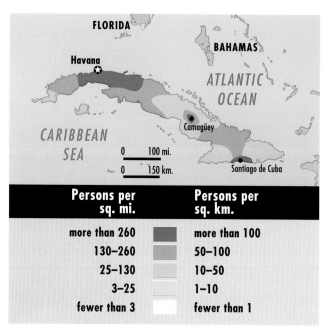

Persons per sq. mi.		Persons per sq. km.
more than 260		more than 100
130–260		50–100
25–130		10–50
3–25		1–10
fewer than 3		fewer than 1

Population distribution in Cuba

Most recently, Cuba has been a haven for Latin American political refugees, particularly from countries such as Chile and Nicaragua, which have had their own kinds of social revolution. Castro has supported their efforts and provided a refuge when necessary.

Who Lives in Cuba?

Mulattoes	51%
Whites	37%
Blacks	11%
Other	1%

Discrimination

The absence of European women in Cuba led to mixed marriages between European men and black women, producing the mixed race, or mulattoes, of Cuba today. Official Cuban statistics still put white people in the majority, but most people seem to disagree.

Schoolchildren proudly hold up their art.

A man from Trinidad
weaving baskets

The general view is that well over half the people of Cuba today are mulattoes. This should not be surprising, however. Since the Revolution, approximately 1 million white people have left Cuba. Since then, government policies have encouraged the mixing of races. As a result, Cubans are now clearly a "browner" race than they were before the Revolution.

In many respects there is almost total racial equality in Cuba today. People get on well together, are friendly and hospitable and share the same sense of fun. They marry irrespective of color, and although there may be some family disapproval if a white girl marries a black man, it is mostly because her economic prospects may not be as good.

In the workplace, there is some distinction. Many blacks and mulattoes work as teachers, but few have top administrative or legal positions. It is also noticeable that whites get the

Population of Major Cities (est. 1993)	
Havana (right)	2,175,995
Santiago de Cuba	440,084
Camagüey	293,961
Holguín	242,085
Guantánamo	207,796
Santa Clara	205,400

better jobs in tourist resorts and hotels. While the lighter-skinned men and women work at the reception desks or serve in the restaurants, their black co-workers are usually cleaning rooms or working in the kitchens.

Working Women

Castro's government also decided that women should be given the opportunity to play an equal part in building the socialist state. They had, after all, fought alongside men in the Rebel Army and were strong supporters of the Revolution. Today, Cuban women make up about 40 percent of the workforce. Many work as teachers, lawyers, and doctors, but few have made it to the top positions.

The state encourages women to work by providing preschool facilities where children from the age of six

A woman worker sieving building sand

months are cared for while their mothers work. Even more progressive was the legislation in the Family Code passed in 1974, in which the responsibilities of married couples are spelled out. Men are instructed to do their half share in bringing up the children and doing the housework. The Cuban Women's Federation played a prominent part in preparing the legislation.

The new role for women does not, however, mean that men have become less *macho* (driven by exaggerated masculinity). They still express their masculinity by whistling at a good-looking woman or making comments, most of which are taken as a compliment or a joke. Men also believe they have

Children and their day care provider playing market at a day care center in Havana

every right to be unfaithful to their wives. The revolutionary government encourages marriage, and weddings have doubled since the Revolution. Unfortunately, divorce has risen at much the same rate, and currently about 60 percent of people between the ages of twenty-five and forty have been divorced at least once.

The Cuban Language

Spanish is the national language of Cuba and is spoken everywhere on the island. Cubans can be difficult to understand because they often drop the final letters off words and run one word into the next. Also, some consonants in Spanish have different sounds than they do in English, or do not exist at all in English.

Pronunciation

c	sounds like "k." But before an "i" or "e," "c" sounds like the "s" in "some"
d	sounds like "th"
g	sounds like "h" before "i" or "e"
h	silent
j	is a strong, guttural sound not found in English, like a throaty "h"
ll	sounds like "y" in yawn
ñ	sounds like "ny" in canyon
r	is "rr-oled" at the beginning of a word
rr	is strongly "rrr-oled"
v	sounds like "b," so *vino* (wine) is pronounced "be-no"
z	sounds like the "s" in "sun"

Stress

If a word ends in a vowel, or in "n" or "s," the next-to-last syllable is stressed; for example, *zapato* (shoe) is pronounced sa-PA-toe

If a word ends in a consonant other than "n" or "s," the last syllable is stressed; for example, *decidir* (to decide) is pronounced day-si-DEAR

If a word is to be stressed in any different way, an acute accent is written over the vowel to be stressed; for example, *máquina* (machine), *Atlántico* (Atlantic Ocean), *jamón* (ham).

The tugboat *Dr. Daniels* heads for Key West's naval pier filled with 700 to 900 people in 1980.

Alina Fernández Revuelta, Fidel Castro's daughter, in a demonstration against her father in New York at the United Nations, 1995.

Escaping from Cuba

Most of the Cubans who have fled since the Revolution have settled in Florida. The first 200,000 or so to leave included many landowners and businesspeople who realized that they would not be able to continue their affluent lifestyle under the new regime. In 1965, Castro let others go if they were not needed for military service. A year later, the U.S. government passed an act allowing Cuban immigrants automatic entry to the United States.

Another 125,000 people left Cuba in 1980. This started as a small incident when a dozen dissidents forced their way into the Peruvian Embassy in Havana and asked for asylum. When another 10,000 Cubans decided they too wanted to go, President Jimmy Carter added to Castro's embarrassment by virtually issuing an open invitation to any Cuban. Castro reacted by opening the port of Mariel on the north coast and allowing anyone to leave who wished to do so. He also used this opportunity to get rid of thousands of prisoners and dissidents, though the U.S. government did not realize this until later.

There was no other large exodus until 1994. But there were some enterprising, single-handed escapes, including a pilot who hijacked his own plane flying tourists from Varadero to Havana; and Castro's daughter, Alina, who fled by way of Spain disguised as a tourist. She was followed a year later by Castro's granddaughter. In addition, various athletes, dancers, and musicians have defected while overseas on official business.

Cuban emigrants aboard a raft headed for Florida

The most dramatic and dangerous way to leave is by sea from northern Cuba to the Florida Keys. This has been the only way open to most Cubans, who have risked their lives in precarious homemade rafts. Many set off on nothing more than the inner tubes of truck tires, a sail made from sacks, a pair of oars, some basic provisions—and sometimes, life jackets. Some were unaware of the hazards of strong winds, sharks, thirst, and hunger during the long weeks at sea. Only about half of the people who set out in these rafts are thought to have made it to safety.

Even so, when the economic situation in Cuba was at rock bottom in 1994, thousands were undeterred. However, this time the United States did not open its doors. Instead, the government reversed its 1966 act and no longer gave Cubans automatic asylum. Many of the "rafters," or *balseros* as they are known, were forced to return to the Guantánamo base, where they had to stay until their legal applications for entry to the United States could be processed.

Common Spanish Phrases

Hay/No hay	There is/There is not
¿Cuánto cuesta?	What does it cost?
¿Dónde está . . . ?	Where is. . . ?
Me gustaría . . .	I would like . . .
Mucho gusto	I am pleased to meet you
Hablo muy poco español	I speak very little Spanish
Buenos días	Good day

Compañero and *Compañera* are used by Cubans instead of the more formal *Señor* and *Señora*.

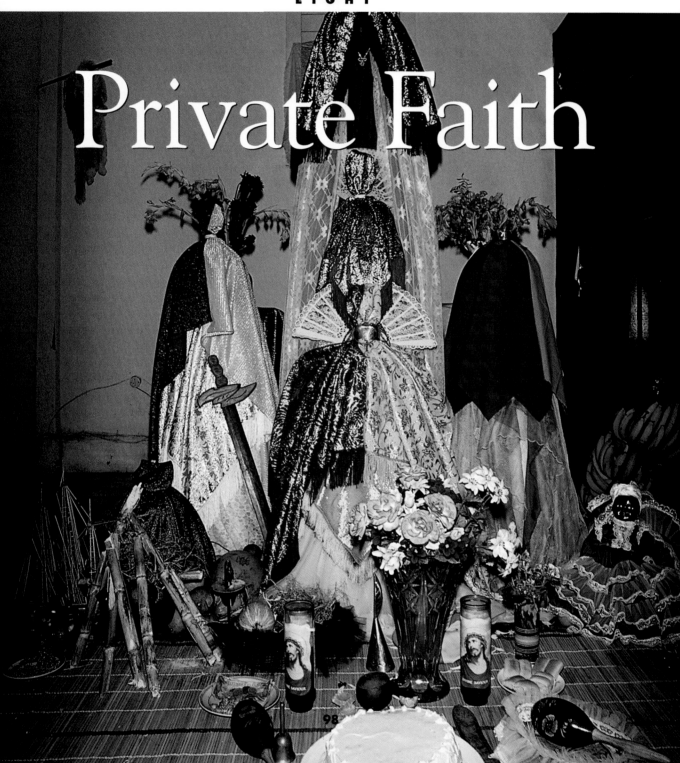

Private Faith

In January 1998, Pope John Paul II made a historic visit to Cuba. It was the first visit by any pope to a country that is often seen as having no religious faith. Crowds gathered and waved flags as the pope's motorcade passed. Not everybody who saw the pope was Roman Catholic because Cuba is a land of many faiths. Of the almost 12 million population, only about 900,000 attend a church service on Sundays. Just over half of those are Catholics, and the rest belong to various evangelical groups.

Opposite: **An altar to the orishas, or African gods, of the Santería religion**

Pope John Paul II arrives at Havana's José Martí airport on January 1, 1998.

Religions of Cuba*

Santería, or Ocha Rule

Conga Rule, or
    Palo Mayombe

Roman Catholic

Protestant and Evangelical

Others, including Spiritism

*A percentage breakdown of people following specific religions is not available.

A Mixture of Faiths

Most of Cuba's people are followers of non-Christian faiths or simply have no religion at all. Although precise figures are hard to determine, a religion that is a mixture of traditional African beliefs and Christianity is probably the most popular in Cuba. Many people practice their faith privately, not because it is prohibited, but because they have a very close relationship with their personal higher power. Such a private communion is something Cubans and many other people in the world today still treasure.

The Roman Catholic Church

When the first Europeans arrived in Cuba, the American Indian inhabitants had many beliefs connected with the natural world around them. Both good and evil spirits abounded in the countryside and all of them were given offerings. Priests practiced magic, and held power over the people by knowing how to please the gods.

The Spanish brought their own Roman Catholic faith to the island. They built churches, including Havana's fine cathedral. For more than 400 years, the Catholic Church and the men that ruled the island built up a strong political unit. Catholicism remained the religion of the wealthier people, while many of the poor, especially the slaves, kept to their own belief system.

With the Revolution of 1959, new administrators and special councils were set up. Catholicism was effectively replaced by the ideology of Communism. Catholics were not allowed to join the Communist Party. Today, twelve bishops care for the spiritual needs of half a million Cubans. Various orders of the Catholic Church continue their work, including Franciscans, Salesians, and Jesuits. Fidel Castro was himself educated in a Jesuit college, and in 1996 he went to Rome to extend a personal invitation to Pope John Paul II to visit Cuba.

The Columbus Cemetery

The story of Cuba's Catholic history is told in the great Columbus cemetery in Havana—*El Cementerio Colón*. The cemetery covers 138 acres (56 ha) and contains the tombs of thousands of people—some humble, some famous. The cemetery was designed by Spanish architect Calixti Aureliano Loira, and the first stone was laid in 1871.

Today, the entire area is covered with tombs, mostly made of fine marble. The cemetery is often described as an open-air museum. The wealthiest families erected enormous tombs or mausoleums, their size reflecting the family's status. Some resemble Grecian temples complete with marble columns. One of the most famous tombs is dedicated to the firemen who died in Havana's great fire of 1890. Another, visited by dozens of people daily, is known as *La Milagrosa* (The Miraculous One). It is the tomb of Amelia Goyri de Hoz, who was credited with miraculous healing powers.

Cubans celebrate the fiesta of African gods called the Day of Kings, or *Guemillere*.

African Gods

Slaves from Africa brought their native religions to Cuba. Central to the Yoruba religion was a supreme being whom the Yoruba believed was surrounded by many gods. To his right, more than 400 gods, or *orishas*, worked for the well-being of the people. To his left, more than 200 other orishas worked evil.

As if to add strength to their beliefs, the African slaves were kept in pitiful conditions. Apart from compulsory Christian baptism and learning a few prayers, they were left to their own ways. Although the slaves never had the opportunity to join the

Pilgrimage to Saint Lazarus

December 17 is the feast day of the Christian Saint Lazarus, the brother of Martha and Mary. Lazarus was a close friend of Jesus. The traditions of Lazarus were carried to Cuba by Spaniards, and a church was built in his honor at El Rincón, a small village outside Havana.

The church known as the *Santuario de San Lázaro* is the focus of an immense pilgrimage. In December, 50,000 people or more converge on the sanctuary. Most come on foot, but some ride bicycles, some travel in old cars or in the few buses, and some even shuffle on bended knee. The route to El Rincón is lined with stalls where people sell candles and homemade snacks. There is a spirit of devotion mixed with fun.

At the church, candles are lit and prayers offered to Saint Lazarus, in the image of a black saint. In the eyes of the pilgrims, the saint is seen as Babalú Ayé, the Yoruba orisha of illness. Many people make offerings of food or money and then rely on the orisha to cure them. The night of December 16 is devoted to the orisha and December 17 to Saint Lazarus, though it is difficult to separate the two.

---

ruling Catholic section of Cuban society, they found peace with the European saints because they seemed to have the same role as their orishas.

Some slaves managed to buy their freedom, and they tended to move to the towns. They established their own communities and their own religion, known as *Santería* or *Ocha Rule*. Santería is a mixture of African beliefs in the powers of orishas with the love of a saint. At the heart of the religion are the *babalwayos*, priests who help followers to communicate with the orishas. Many of the ceremonies are private and involve advice on how to keep the orishas happy. Simple offerings of food are part of most ceremonies, but occasionally an animal such as a chicken or goat is sacrificed. A Santería festival is accompanied by music, drumming, dances, food, and drink.

Slaves from other parts of West Africa brought other religions. People from the Congo River area who were of Bantu origin revered sacred symbols identifying the spirits or orishas.

Santa Bárbara

According to a legend handed down over the centuries, Santa Bárbara was the daughter of a pagan, a non-Christian named Dioscoro from Nicomedia in ancient Greece. When Bárbara converted to the Christian faith, her father handed her over to the local authorities, who executed her. Her martyrdom for her beliefs led to sainthood, and Santa Bárbara is venerated every year on December 4, her feast day. Prayers are said to her as a protection against such misfortunes as thunderstorms and fire. She is worshiped as the Patron Saint of Firemen and the Artillery—the soldiers who fire large guns. In Cuba, Santa Bárbara is also seen as the orisha Changó. This orisha is favored because it is connected with many affairs from war to music, dance, and youthfulness. Changó represents the greatest number of human virtues and faults, so daily prayers are said at the shrine and small offerings of local foods are left on plates.

A Santería master standing next to a shrine in his home

This religion, which includes elements of the Catholic religion, has survived as the *Conga Rule* or *Palo Mayombe*.

The Daily Prayer

The orishas are so much a part of the Cuban way of life that many people have their favorites. With a huge number of orishas and their parallel saints, there is a seemingly endless choice. Many Cuban homes have a small shrine somewhere, often set in a corner. It may be decorated with a white cloth, perhaps some flowers, family photos, and a small image of a saint. Santa Bárbara is one of the most popular.

The Spirit of Christmas Past

After the Revolution, the Catholic Church and its political followers suddenly had a very lowly place in Cuban life. The church was not banned, nor was it supported. For many years religion passed into the wilderness, the Christian faith especially. Churches fell into ruin or were taken over, and few people attended mass. At the time of the Revolution, there were Protestant groups in Cuba, including many evangelical sects. The new government required these groups to be registered, and at the time the registry was closed in the late 1960s, about fifty were listed.

In the mid-1980s, after publication in Havana of Fidel Castro's conversations with Frei Betto, a Brazilian priest, attitudes softened. The atmosphere also changed when support from the Soviet Union ceased and the Cuban government had to introduce the Special Period austerity plan. Many people sought comfort from religious faith, and Santería especially saw a tremendous revival. Christian congregations also increased. The pope's visit in early 1998 was timely. The economy was improving, and with the announcement of the pope's imminent arrival, the government was able to announce the revival of Christmas.

Important Religious Holidays

Procession of the Miracles	December 17
Christmas	December 25

For the first time since the Revolution, Cubans were authorized to celebrate Christmas in 1997. Many chose that day to get married at the government-run palace of matrimony.

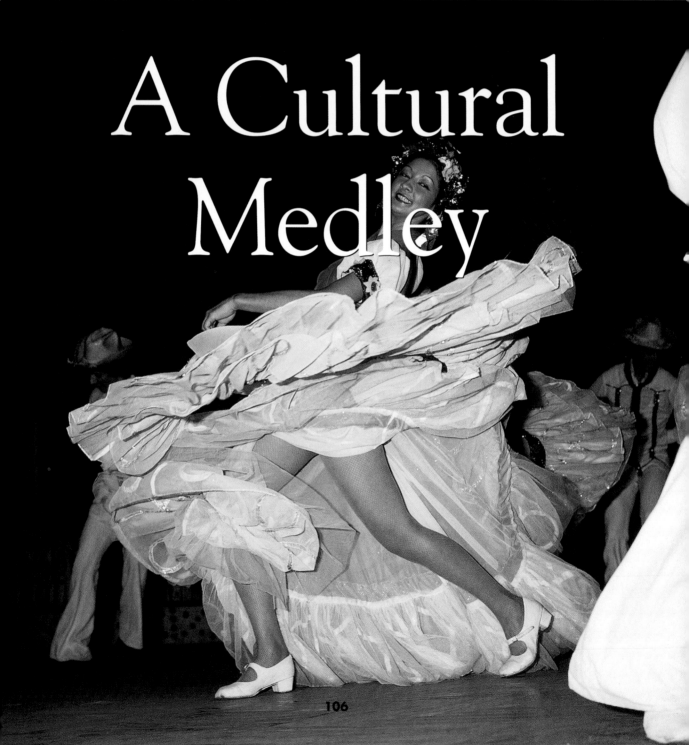

A Cultural Medley

The *Gran Teatro* in Havana

W
HEN CASTRO CAME to power in 1959, he wanted to make culture available to the mass of ordinary Cubans. The government poured money into building museums, galleries, art schools, and theaters in all the major towns. It established a film industry, and guaranteed salaries to Afro-Cuban groups, top musicians, and other artists. But many of Cuba's foremost intellectuals and artists left Cuba, fearing that they would lose the freedom to pursue their own ideas. Those who remained have had to learn to work within the government's political doctrines.

Revolutionary Culture

In the early years, the theater, and especially the cinema, were used to spread propaganda and revolutionary ideals. Since then, the government appears to have mellowed and has allowed films like *Fresa y Chocolate* (*Strawberry and Chocolate*), which openly criticizes the government while telling a story of homosexuality, a subject that was once banned. In the past, the revolutionary government sent hundreds of homosexuals to labor camps.

Opposite: **A cabaret dancer at the Tropicana in Havana**

A Cultural Medley **107**

The Museum of the City of Havana

On one side of the Plaza de Armas, the central square of Old Havana, stands the fine baroque building known as the Palace of the Captains-General. Built between 1776 and 1791, it was the home of Cuba's colonial governors.

Today, it houses the Museum of the City of Havana. From the street, which is said to have been made of wood so as not to disturb the captain-general's sleep, you enter a small courtyard. Below the courtyard are tunnels through which the city's water once flowed. To one side is a room containing a fine selection of eighteenth-century religious art.

On the second floor, a number of rooms take you through Cuba's history. First are the uniforms of the colonial army, their weapons, and a leather cannon made by rebels. Next comes a display of portraits of all the independence fighters and some of their possessions, including Antonio Maceo's boat and his machete, and Máximo Gómez's death mask. You then move on to the fight against imperialism and the Batista regime, including a huge exhibit of some broken pieces from the U.S.S. *Maine* monument.

The most impressive room, part of the colonial period, is the throne room of the king of Spain (above). Furnished in red and gold, there are fine ceramics, large golden candleholders, paintings, and some colonial furniture. The room was kept ready should the king ever come to visit. He never did.

Since the Special Period began, however, many theaters have closed and film production has been cut back. However, the government has ensured that the New Latin American Film Festival, hosted by Havana every year since 1979, has continued. It is the most prestigious film festival in the Spanish-speaking world and attracts actors, directors, and producers from many countries.

Cuban Music and Dance

Cubans are natural musicians; they love to play, sing, and dance. Their music has Spanish and African roots, "a love affair between the African drum and the Spanish guitar," to quote a famous Cuban musician. Slowly, over the centuries, the two blended. By the end of the nineteenth century they were merged in the romantic *habanera* and the sensuous *danzón*.

The lively rumba emerged toward the end of the 1800s from black communities in Matanzas and Havana, taking the whites by storm. An Afro-Cuban dance style based on drum rhythms, it is associated with the black religious practices of Santería. There are different forms of rumba—the slow *yambú* performed in pairs, the faster *guaguancó*, and the fast and acrobatic *columbia*.

Son is another rhythm with black origins. The usual instrumentation was a sextet of guitar, *tres*, double bass, bongo, maracas, claves, and singers, but the music was later adapted to orchestras with large percussion sections and horns. Beny Moré was Cuba's most famous son singer. A legend in his time, he was nicknamed "The Barbarian of Rhythm" and was greatly mourned when he died in 1963 at the age of forty-three.

National Ballet

A major success story since the Revolution has been the National Ballet of Cuba, founded by the remarkable Alicia Alonso. Alonso is now in her seventies and is affectionately dubbed "the First Lady of Cuba." She studied in Cuba and New York and in 1948 helped to found the *Ballet de Cuba*, which became known as the *Ballet Nacional de Cuba* after 1959. Close associations with the Kirov and Bolshoi Ballets of the Soviet Union led to successful and internationally acclaimed tours. In Havana, the National Ballet performs in the ornate *Gran Teatro*. Its repertoire includes classical and modern ballets as well as productions by Cuban masters.

After the son came the mambo, made famous in the 1950s by band leader Pérez Prado, the cha-cha-chá, and, more recently, the very popular salsa, which is son combined with all of these plus other Latin American rhythms and a touch of jazz. One of the greatest salsa singers is Celia Cruz, who left Cuba in the early 1960s.

An Afro-Cuban music group playing their decorated instruments

Today in Cuba, Los Van Van, founded in 1969, is one of the most popular bands. It has created its own sound, *songo*, which combines trombones and violins with jazz harmonies and call-and-response lyrics. Another top band is Irakere, founded by the brilliant pianist "Chucho" Valdés, whose American-style jazz combined with Afro-Cuban percussion has deep son roots. NG La Banda has been a hit since it started in 1989. The Afro-Cuban All

Stars perform Cuban big-band classics from the 1940s and 1950s. The thirteen-piece, multigenerational band is popular in Cuba and abroad.

In some Cuban towns there is a *casa de trova*, where guitar players sing old songs in traditional style. The tradition of singing ballads and protest songs goes back a long way and was revived in the 1970s. Two of the most popular performers of *nueva trova*, as it is known, are Silvio Rodríguez and Pablo Milanés. Initially they were not tolerated by the revolutionary government, but they have now been accepted.

Literature

Two of Cuba's great writers during the twentieth century were the mulatto poets Nicolás Guillén (1902–1989) and Alejo Carpentier (1904–1980), a diplomat and journalist. Before the Revolution, both spent many years in exile. They wrote most of their best works before 1959. Carpentier wrote with a surreal mix of fact and fiction and among his best-known works are *The Kingdom of the World* and *Explosion in a Cathedral*. Guillén fought in the Spanish Civil War and became a Communist. He wrote many poems praising the Revolution's achievements and became Cuba's national poet. Both men drew inspiration from Afro-Cuban culture, as did Miguel Barnet, Cuba's leading modern writer. His best-known book is *The Autobiography of a Runaway Slave*.

Alejo Carpentier (1904–1980), Cuban poet and journalist

Wilfredo Lam

Cuba's famous artist Wilfredo Lam was born of unusual parents. His father was a Chinese shopkeeper who had settled in Cuba, and his mother was a mulatto with some American Indian blood. Lam was the youngest of eight children, and his father was eighty-four years old when Lam was born. The family was reasonably prosperous, and Lam was educated in Havana and then in Spain. He fought in the Spanish Civil War and in 1938 moved to France, where he was greatly influenced by Picasso and the surrealists. The outbreak of World War II in 1939 forced him to return to Cuba.

"My first impression when I returned to Havana . . . was one of terrible sadness. . . . Havana at that time was a land of pleasure, of sugary music, mambas, rumbas, and so forth. The Negroes were considered picturesque. They themselves aped the whites and regretted that they did not have light skins." Lam's reaction to these observations was to produce probably his greatest work, *The Great Jungle*, which now hangs in the Museum of Modern Art in New York.

Lam was a fierce opponent of Batista and returned to Europe in 1952. He welcomed the Castro regime and from Paris helped organize exhibitions in Cuba and at the Havana Cultural Congress of 1968. After that, his relations with the revolutionary government deteriorated, and he spent the remaining years of his life with his Swedish wife in Genoa, Italy.

Quinceañera

A very important date for young people in Cuba, and in much of Latin America, is the day they become fifteen years old. The fifteenth birthday represents a "coming-of-age" when young people enter adulthood and are considered ready for marriage. Parents invite family and friends to a party. Wealthier families may celebrate in a fancy hotel with a dinner, followed by dancing. Girls wear elegant dresses especially made for the occasion, and boys wear their best suits and ties. Even during the Special Period, families have maintained this tradition.

Sport

After the Revolution, Fidel Castro made sports a top priority in all Cuban schools. Children who showed athletic talent were sent to special schools. The government provides facilities for virtually all the sports that are played in North America and Europe. In Cuba, however, sports are played on an amateur basis. Top athletes do not earn huge sums of money, although some are funded completely by the state. So Cuban children are always reminded that they must keep up with their studies as well as their sports.

The emphasis placed on sports has paid off, and Cuba has been a principal medal-winner in many Central American and Pan-American Games, as well as the Olympics. In the 1991 Pan-American Games, despite great economic difficulties at home, Cuba became the first Latin American country to win more gold medals than the United States. The sports in which Cuba has particularly excelled are boxing, basketball, track and field, and volleyball.

Cuba's Félix Savon poses with his gold medal for the 201 pound (91 kg) heavyweight class of Olympic boxing at the Olympic Games in Atlanta, Georgia, 1996.

Sports Heroes

Enrique Figuerola, a 100-meter sprinter, won Cuba's first Olympic medal—a silver—in the 1964 Tokyo Games.

Teófilo Stevenson is the only heavyweight boxer to have won three gold Olympic medals (1972, 1976, 1980).

Alberto Juantorena was the first athlete to win gold medals in both the 400 and 800 meters in the Olympics (1976).

Ana Fidelia Quirot was the Pan-American and Olympic champion in the 800 meters. Despite suffering serious burns in a fire, she recovered in a year and a half to win the silver medal in the 800 meters in the Atlanta Olympics in 1996.

Javier Sotomayor, the Olympic and Pan-American high-jump champion, still holds the world record of 8 feet (2 m).

María Caridad Colón in the Moscow Olympic Games in 1980 became the first Latin American woman to win a gold medal for the javelin.

Baseball

Baseball was introduced into Cuba in 1865 from the United States by some American students. The first baseball clubs were founded in Havana and Matzanas in 1872, and their first match took place in December 1874, with Havana winning 59–9. The first official championships were held in 1878. For a time, the Spanish authorities banned the game. They associated it with the fight for Cuban independence because money from baseball matches was used to support the rebels. After Independence, with many U.S. Marines still in the country, baseball became even more popular, especially among young people. Cuba entered a baseball team in the Central American Games for the first time in 1926—and won the championship.

Today, baseball is Cuba's national sport, and children play it almost as soon as they can walk. The Baseball National Series takes place among the fourteen provinces every year between November and January. Teams are named after a town or region—for example, the Metropolitanos are from

Havana. Others are associated with industries, such as the Azucareros (sugar workers) from Villa Clara and the Tabacaleros (tobacco workers) from Pinar del Río. Hundreds of thousands of supporters follow the matches. So many people stop work to watch the final match of the series on television or listen on the radio that the country comes to a virtual standstill.

In March 1999, the Baltimore Orioles traveled to Havana to play Cuba's national all-star team in the first of two exhibition matches. This was the first time since 1959 that a U.S. major league team played in Cuba. The Cubans lost 3–2, but they won the May 1999 rematch in Baltimore 12–6.

Members of the Cuban baseball team carry their flag around the field after defeating Japan at the Summer Olympics in Atlanta.

A Taste of Life

An oxen-drawn sledge
loaded with agricultural
produce

The Special Period introduced in 1991 has been very
difficult for many Cubans, most of all in their efforts to get
enough food for the family. Long lines outside shops are part
of everyday life and form quickly when news of a food deliv-
ery gets around. In towns, there are even lines for such basics
as bread and milk, while people in the countryside are a little
more fortunate. In some villages, bread is delivered by horse
and cart, while milk arrives daily by truck and is rationed out
from the village store.

Opposite: **A group of
secondary level students**

A Taste of Life   **117**

Independent market traders selling *malanga, boniato,* and *yuca* (left to right)

Basic foods in Cuba are rice, beans, *yuca* (manioc or cassava), *boniato* (a sweet potato), and *malanga*, a root vegetable, as well as citrus fruits like grapefruit and oranges, and bananas and plantains. People in the countryside get a greater variety of fruit, including avocado, mango, papaya, and pineapple. These are available in private markets in the towns, but at high prices. Cubans eat eggs, chicken, and pork when they can get them, but beef is a luxury. People are sent to prison for eight years for illegally killing a cow.

Despite their country's extensive coastline, Cubans eat very little fish. In the 1960s, Castro attempted to add large amounts of fish to the Cuban diet. His attempt failed because, historically, fish was considered to be "slave food" and therefore unacceptable. This is similar to the historical rejection of catfish in the United States.

National Holidays in Cuba

Liberation Day	January 1
Victory Day	January 2
José Martí's Birthday	January 28
Anniversary of the Second War of Independence	February 24
International Women's Day	March 8
Anniversary of the Students' Attack on the Presidential Palace	March 13
Bay of Pigs Victory	April 19
Labor Day	May 1
National Revolution Day	July 26
Day of the Martyrs of the Revolution	July 30
Anniversary of Che Guevara's Death	October 8
Memorial Day for Camilio Cienfuegos	October 28
Anniversary of the Landing of the *Granma*	December 2
Memorial Day for Antonio Maceo	December 7

Cuban food is not spicy, but garlic, peppers, and onions are common ingredients. *Ajiaco* is a typical stew made of meat, garlic, and vegetables, and *picadillo* is a dish of shredded beef mixed with green peppers, onions, tomatoes, and olives. Sometimes a sauce of lemon and garlic, called *mojo*, is served with vegetables. *Fufu* is boiled and mashed plantains generally served with meat. And everything comes with rice.

A National Dish

The closest thing to a national dish in Cuba is *moros y cristianos* or *congrí* which is very similar. *Moros y cristianos* (Moors and Christians) refers to the Moors, or Muslim Arabs, who invaded Spain centuries ago. The dish is sometimes compared to the racial mix in Cuba itself: white rice and black beans cooked together with onions, garlic, green pepper, tomatoes, salt, and pepper. Sometimes an egg is served with the rice. *Congrí* is rice cooked with red kidney beans. It was introduced by French planters from Haiti during the nineteenth century.

At the time of the Revolution, people who were renting properties or paying mortgages were given their houses and apartments. Revolutionary officials took over some of the houses confiscated from Cubans who left the country. After the Revolution, the government got rid of the shanty slums that surrounded Havana and some other large towns, and built prefabricated high-rise apartment blocks, similar to those in the Soviet Union and Eastern Europe. Rents were very low, about 10 percent of a person's salary, and installment plans enabled people to buy a home.

Since 1970, much of the new construction has been done by "microbrigades," small groups of men and women of various trades and professions. They work together under expert guidance to build housing blocks, and they get first priority if they want an apartment. There has been less new construction in the Special Period because building materials have been unavailable.

A run-down mansion on the Malecón houses many families.

The Special Period is not the only reason for these problems. People moving out of rural areas have put enormous pressure on housing in towns. Almost three-fourths of Cuba's people now live in urban areas, with one-fifth of the population in Havana alone. There, in large mansions once owned by the wealthy, many families crowd into converted

Going to Work

Since the Special Period began, with gasoline in very short supply, the most popular way of getting about has been by bicycle. Most towns are filled with crowds of cyclists going to and from work. Even on isolated roads, cyclists can be seen covering long distances. Few people own cars, but old Cadillacs, Chevrolets, and others are still widely used, especially as taxis.

The few public buses are dangerously overcrowded, and pickup trucks sometimes take their place. Other kinds of transport include horse-drawn cabs, tricycles that carry passengers, and a human-drawn cart similar to a rickshaw. Havana has *camellos*, so called because the long, two-truck vehicles resemble camels. They carry up to 250 people, and the fare, no matter what the distance, is only 20 centavos.

apartments. Often, three generations live in a two- or three-room apartment with a tiny kitchen and toilet. Every day in the Special Period, electricity and water supplies are cut off, often for several hours.

No one has money to spend on the upkeep of the apartments, and the mansions are gradually falling into ruins. Even for families lucky enough to be paid in U.S. dollars, it is an uphill struggle, with both parents often working at more than one job to make ends meet.

Cubans are justifiably proud of their country's education record since the Revolution. In 1958 there were almost 1 million illiterate people in Cuba, and over two-thirds of the rural population had no schools.

In 1961, Castro closed all schools in Cuba for eight months and sent 250,000 students and teachers into rural areas to teach people how to read and write. By the end of 1962, the illiteracy rate had dropped from 24 percent to 4 percent. Old military headquarters and police stations were converted into schools, and thousands of volunteers built new ones. Now education is free for everyone from kindergarten to university, and the 95 percent literacy level is among the highest in developing countries.

Cuban children go to primary school from age 5 to age 11 or 12, and to secondary school until they are 17. The state normally provides all transport, textbooks, equipment, and school meals, but the Special Period has brought severe shortages in everything. Schoolchildren wear red and white uniforms at the primary level and yellow and white uniforms at the secondary level. School attendance is high—almost 100 percent at primary level—and Cuba has one of the highest teacher-student ratios in the world, about 1 to 39 as compared to 1 to 77 in the United States.

Scholarships are available for students to go to boarding schools, which helps those living far from a school. Cuba also has special sports schools, where students with obvious talent in sports can train and receive their education. Whether or not they are successful at the international level, most continue as physical education instructors in Cuba. Students with artistic talent can attend vocational arts schools, where tuition in music, ballet, modern dance, and visual arts is combined with conventional studies. Special schools, as well as facilities for one-to-one teaching in ordinary schools, help children with learning disabilities.

Girls practicing their ballet steps

Students going on to higher education have a choice of eight universities and nearly fifty institutes of higher education. In addition, vocational schools offer courses in agriculture, industry, and technology.

Children work together in their school garden.

Cuba's hero José Martí believed in linking education with the country's agriculture, and in 1970 the Cuban government created "The School in the Country," where students divide their time between the classroom and the fields. Its objective is to make students aware of their social responsibilities, and to reduce prejudice against manual labor.

"José Martí" Pioneers

At holiday time, weekends, and after school, children gather in the Pioneers Palace of their town to take part in various activities. They belong to the 2-million-strong "José Martí" Pioneers, or *Pioneros*, the most important children's organization in Cuba. It was created to encourage children to study, work, and take pride in the history of their country.

Many adult volunteers help run the organization, which encourages sports, culture, and recreation. The organization also runs scientific and technical clubs and encourages children to take part in community activities that will help their neighbors and the state.

Enith Alerm Prieto, a 28-year-old industrial engineer, is the current president of the Pioneers organization. She is also the Council of State's youngest member and a National Assembly deputy.

Health Care

Along with education, the revolutionary government's principal aim has been to provide good medical treatment for all Cubans. Before 1959, Cuban health care was advanced but almost two-thirds of all doctors, dentists, nurses, and chemists lived in or around Havana. Small towns and rural areas had few hospitals and little available medical treatment. After the Revolution, almost two-thirds of the island's 6,000 doctors left Cuba.

One of the revolutionary government's first actions was to set up training programs for tens of thousands of doctors. Part of their training was and still is to spend two years in the rural health program. Hospitals and polyclinics were built. Polyclinics are half-hospital and half-clinic, with a resident doctor and nurse who can be called on after working hours if necessary. Most housing projects, apartment blocks, neighborhoods, and villages have one, often built by voluntary labor.

Part of the work of the polyclinics is to provide vaccinations. In the last thirty years, malaria and tetanus have been eradicated and other diseases including tuberculosis and meningitis have been reduced. In 1962, Cuba became the first country to be free of polio. Vaccinations continue to be given regularly against diphtheria, whooping cough, smallpox, and measles.

Now Cuba has 292 hospitals, 63,000 doctors, and nearly 10,000 dentists. There is one doctor for every 270 inhabitants—a better ratio than that in the United States—and treatment is free for everyone. The infant mortality rate is 7.3 per 1,000, one of the lowest in the world, and life expectancy is 76 years. Cuba's health program has been so successful that many people come from abroad for specialized treatment, which is good for the economy because it brings in extra dollars. Victims of Russia's 1986 Chernobyl nuclear disaster have been treated in Cuba, and Cuban emergency medical teams help other nations after hurricanes and other disasters.

A group of medical students in Santiago de Cuba

The Special Period of the 1990s has put a great deal of pressure on the health service, however. There are insufficient funds for wages and equipment, standards in the hospitals and clinics have fallen, and there is a serious shortage of medicines. To help the people and the economy, Cuban specialists have turned back the clock and are increasingly using natural medicines. Schools and other centers have been encouraged to grow herb gardens filled with medicinal plants.

A street scene during the
Santiago de Cuba festival

Time Off

Few Cubans can afford to take time off. In better days, they used to go to the coast for holidays to enjoy the beaches, swimming, and diving. Now there is no transport to the coast, and the best beaches are reserved for tourists.

Cubans love movies and will line up for hours to see a new release. They also enjoy the theater, but productions of both have been seriously curtailed, and many families now pass the evening watching television.

Cubans are essentially happy, carefree people who will make the most of any occasion or party. Many national holidays are marked with long political speeches delivered by Fidel Castro or his brother Raúl. In Havana these take place in the huge *Plaza de la Revolución*, dominated by a towering monument to José Martí and a large metal sculpture of Che Guevara. The Cuban people enjoy these occasions, which they celebrate with their families. The mood is festive and the party goes on well into the night.

Young couples dance in the streets as the annual Carnival celebration begins on the island.

Timeline

Cuban History

Ciboney people arrive in Cuba.	**About 3500 B.C.– A.D. 1200**
Taíno people arrive in Cuba.	**About A.D. 1100**
Christopher Columbus lands in Cuba and claims the island for Spain.	1492
Diego Velásquez founds seven *villas*.	1511–1515
Spaniards bring the first African slaves to Cuba.	1520s
Spain allows direct trade between Cuba and the newly independent United States.	1783
Black slaves in Haiti rebel and flee to Cuba.	1791
Cuban revolutionaries fight Spanish rule in the Ten Years' War.	1868–1878
Slavery is abolished in Cuba.	1886
José Martí leads a revolt against Spanish rule.	1895
In the Spanish-American War, the United States supports Cuban revolutionaries and forces Spain to give up its claims to Cuba.	1898

World History

2500 B.C.	Egyptians build the Pyramids and Sphinx in Giza.
563 B.C.	Buddha is born in India.
A.D. 313	The Roman emperor Constantine recognizes Christianity.
610	The prophet Muhammad begins preaching a new religion called Islam.
1054	The Eastern (Orthodox) and Western (Roman) Churches break apart.
1066	William the Conqueror defeats the English in the Battle of Hastings.
1095	Pope Urban II proclaims the First Crusade.
1215	King John seals the Magna Carta.
1300s	The Renaissance begins in Italy.
1347	The Black Death sweeps through Europe.
1453	Ottoman Turks capture Constantinople, conquering the Byzantine Empire.
1492	Columbus arrives in North America.
1500s	The Reformation leads to the birth of Protestantism.
1776	The Declaration of Independence is signed.
1789	The French Revolution begins.
1865	The American Civil War ends.

Cuban History

U.S. military government rules Cuba.	1899–1902
The Republic of Cuba is founded; Tomás Estrada Palma becomes the first president.	1902
The United States establishes a naval base at Guantánamo.	1903
Cuban revolutionary Fulgencio Batista takes control of Cuba's government.	1933
Guerrilla forces of Fidel Castro begin a war against the Cuban government.	1957
Batista flees the country. Castro takes control of the Cuban government.	1959
Castro signs an economic treaty with the Soviet Union and accepts Soviet military aid. The U.S. government places an economic embargo on Cuba.	1960
The U.S. government helps a group of Cuban exiles invade the Bay of Pigs. Castro's forces quickly defeat them.	1961
The United States forces the Soviet Union to remove missiles from Cuba.	1962
Cuba adopts a new Constitution that establishes Cuba as a socialist state with the Communist Party as the only political party.	1976
Castro allows 125,000 Cubans to leave the country, resulting in the Mariel Boatlift to the United States.	1980
Cuba's economy begins to suffer when the Soviet Union collapses.	1991
The government begins economic reforms by allowing some Cubans to start privately owned businesses.	1993
During one month, about 35,000 Cubans flee Cuba in unsafe boats. The United States agrees to accept 20,000 Cuban refugees a year.	1994
Pope John Paul II makes a special trip to Cuba, resulting in more religious freedom for Cubans.	1998

World History

1914	World War I breaks out.
1917	The Bolshevik Revolution brings Communism to Russia.
1929	Worldwide economic depression begins.
1939	World War II begins, following the German invasion of Poland.
1957	The Vietnam War starts.
1989	The Berlin Wall is torn down as Communism crumbles in Eastern Europe.
1996	Bill Clinton re-elected U.S. president.

Fast Facts

Official name: *República de Cuba* (Republic of Cuba)

Capital: Havana

Official language: Spanish

Major religion: None

Punta Gorda

Cuban flag

A bullock cart

Students on the Malecón

Year of founding:	1902
National anthem:	*La Bayamesa (The Bayamo Song)*
Government:	Communist-socialist state with a one-house legislature
Chief of state:	President
Head of government:	President
Area and dimensions:	42,804 square miles (110,861 sq km); 708 miles (1,139 km) northwest to southeast; 135 miles (217 km) north to south
Coordinates of geographic center:	21° 30' North, 80° West
Water borders and nearby land:	The Caribbean Sea to the south and east; the Atlantic Ocean to the northeast; the Straits of Florida to the north; the Gulf of Mexico to the northwest; with nearby land including the Bahamas and the United States (Florida) to the north, Haiti to the southeast, Jamaica to the south, and Mexico to the west
Highest elevation:	Pico Turquino, 6,542 feet (1,994 m)
Lowest elevation:	Sea level along the coast
Average temperature:	70°F (21°C) in January; 80°F (27°C) in July
Average annual precipitation:	More than 70 inches (178 cm) in the mountains; 40 inches (102 cm) in the lowlands
National population (1997 est.):	11,190,000

Near Santiago de Cuba

Tobacco fields

Currency

Population (1993) of largest cities:		
	Havana	2,175,995
	Santiago de Cuba	440,084
	Camagüey	293,961
	Holguín	242,085
	Guantánamo	207,796

Famous landmarks:
- ▶ *Bacanao Park* (Santiago de Cuba)
- ▶ *Cave of the Indians* (Near Viñales)
- ▶ *Indocuban Museum* (Holguín)
- ▶ *Museum of the Festival* (Remedios)
- ▶ *Old City of Havana—castles, churches, museums* (Havana)
- ▶ *Punta del Este Cave Paintings* (Near Punta del Este, Isla de la Juventud)
- ▶ *Romantic Museum* (Trinidad)
- ▶ *Viñales Valley* (Pinar del Río)
- ▶ *Varadero Beach* (North coast of Matanzas Province)
- ▶ *Zapata National Park* (Zapata Peninsula)

Industry: Service industries, such as banking, education, and health, make up the largest part of Cuba's economy. Tourism is Cuba's fastest-growing service industry, with foreign tourists spending about $1 billion per year in Cuba. Manufacturing and mining are important Cuban industries that produce goods. Sugar is Cuba's leading manufactured product. More than 100 sugar mills make refined sugar from Cuban-raised sugarcane. Cigars, oil, food products, cement products, and textiles are other leading manufactured goods. Cuba's leading mineral products are chromite and nickel.

Currency: The Cuban *peso* (CUP) is Cuba's basic monetary unit. Official exchange rate: 1 CUP = $1 U.S. Exchange rate within Cuba: about 23 CUPs = U.S. $1.

Sancti Spíritus

Fidel Castro

Weights and measures:	The metric system with some U.S. and old Spanish measures
Literacy:	95.7 percent (1995 estimate)

Common words and phrases:

Adiós. (ah-dee-OHS)	Goodbye.
Buenos días. (BWAHN-ohs DEE-yahs)	Good day.
Buenas noches. (BWAHN-ohs NOH-chess)	Good evening/night.
Con permiso. (con pair-MEE-so)	With your permission.
¿Cuánto? (KWAHN-toh)	How much?
¿Cuántos? (KWAHN-tohs)	How many?
¿Dónde está . . .? (DOHN-day ess-TAH)	Where is . . . ?
Gracias. (grah-SEE-ahs)	Thank you.
No (noh)	No
por favor (pohr fah-VOHR)	please
¿Qué hora es? (keh O-rah es)	What time is it?
Sí (see)	Yes

Famous Cubans:

Alicia Alonso *Ballerina*	(1921–)
Fulgencio Batista *Dictator*	(1901–1973)
Fidel Castro *Revolutionary and Communist leader*	(1926–)
Nicolás Guillén *National poet*	(1902–1989)
Wilfredo Lam *Painter*	(1902–1982)
José Martí *Political leader and writer*	(1853–1895)
Pérez Prado *Musician*	(1916–)
Teófilo Stevenson *Olympic gold medalist*	(1952–)

To Find Out More

Nonfiction

▶ Ada, Alma Flor. *Under the Royal Palms: A Childhood in Cuba*. New York: Atheneum, 1998.

▶ Crouch, Clifford W. *Cuba*. Broomall, Pa.: Chelsea House, 1997.

▶ Finkelstein, Norman H. *Thirteen Days/Ninety Miles: The Cuban Missile Crisis*. Englewood Cliffs, N.J.: Julian Messner, 1995.

▶ Fox, Mary Virginia. *Cuba*. San Diego: Lucent Books, 1999.

▶ Galvan, Raul. *Cuban Americans*. Tarrytown, N.Y.: Marshall Cavendish, 1995.

▶ Gow, Catherine Hester. *The Cuban Missile Crisis*. San Diego: Lucent Books, 1997.

▶ Haverstock, Nathan A. *Cuba in Pictures*. Minneapolis: Lerner Publications, 1997.

▶ Morrison, Marion. *Cuba*. Orlando, Fla.: Raintree/Steck Vaughn, 1998.

▶ Selsdon, Esther. *The Life and Times of Fidel Castro*. Broomall, Pa.: Chelsea House Publications, 1997.

Websites

▶ **Official Site of the Republic of Cuba**
http://www.cubaweb.cu/
In both Spanish and English, this website includes information on Cuban news, travel, arts and culture, fairs and events, business, science, and government.

▶ **Latin America on the Net**
http://www.latinworld.com/
countries/cuba/
In Spanish and English, this site includes links to reference books, business, culture, the economy, education, politics, and sports in Cuba and other Latin American countries.

▶ **The Cuban Experience**
http://library.advanced.org/18355/
A Web-based educational resource about Cuba, including interactive elements such as forums for discussion, trivia contests, voting booths, simulations, and a search engine.

▶ **Cuba Megalinks**
http://www.lanuevacuba.com
A simple and comprehensive Cuban links website emphasizing articles on Cuba's history.

Organizations and Embassies

Cuban Interests Section
▶ 2630 and 2639 16th Street NW
Washington, D.C. 20009
(202) 797-8518
http://www.embassy.org/embassies/cu.html

Index

Page numbers in *italics* indicate illustrations.

Meet the Author

My LIFE-LONG INTEREST AND INVOLVEMENT WITH Latin America began in the early 1960s. I had studied history and French at university and then traveled to Bolivia as a postgraduate. My touchdown coincided with the tension of the Cuban Missile Crisis, and its news was on everyone's mind. Cuban connections loomed large throughout the region for many years, and I was back in Bolivia on a film-making trip with my husband when the revolutionary Che Guevara was caught.

It was not until the 1990s that I had the chance to visit Cuba for the first time. Changes in the economy were being introduced, and foreign visitors were encouraged to travel to the island. Transport was not always easy, but I managed to

reach many small towns and country settlements. The Spanish I had first learned in Bolivia soon adapted to the local idiom, and I found many people who were happy to tell me about their country. I enjoyed their company, their hospitality and many lively anecdotes.

Once back home in Britain, I found numerous opportunities to rekindle my interest as Cuba's links with Europe strengthened. Many Cuban-oriented events are held throughout Britain, and I follow these closely. My husband and I are members of several nonpolitical organizations involved with Latin America that provide information, contact with universities, and cultural groups. In addition, we have our own collection of books and news clippings.

Photo Credits